Pagan Portals
Ancestral Healing

What people are saying about

Ancestral Healing

An empowering read, this book has a great deal to offer everyone. Human history is full of difficulties we need to deal with, and this anthology, with its many different perspectives and experiences, offers places we can start from. Essential reading for anyone who feels lost or disconnected.
Nimue Brown, author of *Druidry and the Ancestors*

In an era when the ancestors have been ignored, even abandoned, for a millennium or more in the "civilized" western world, it takes a great deal of work to move toward them again, to help them heal and, in the process, to heal ourselves. This anthology offers eleven perspectives on ancestral healing, from the why to the how-to, encompassing blood ancestors, ancestors of spirit, and even ancestral animals. This is a timely work, sharing with the reader the contributors' passion for honoring those who have gone before. It is my fervent hope that their words will inspire more people to work toward ancestral healing.
Laura Perry, editor of *Deathwalking: Helping Them Cross the Bridge* and author of *Ariadne's Thread: Awakening the Wonders of the Ancient Minoans in Our Modern Lives*

This brilliant anthology addresses a core issue for affecting true healing; the weight of the ancestral woundedness we may be carrying. In this book, we are offered insights into these wounds, why we may have carried them in this lifetime, and how we can heal. The reader is treated to wisdom in understanding our place in familial constellations and how to shine our own divine light brightly. Each contributor in this anthology shares their expertise with compassion and caring, inspiring the reader to look deeply within to step out of limiting beliefs or diseases carried in the blood of our ancestors.

Janet Elizabeth Gale, author of *The Rush Hour Shaman*

It is becoming increasingly recognised that when a traumatic event is experienced the effects of it, the post traumatic stress if you will, is still being carried many generations later. Therefore one of the most powerful things we can do for ourself and for future generations, is to carry out ancestral healing in some form. Knowing how to go about this can be difficult to discover but in this inspiring and much needed anthology eleven authors share their perspectives on ancestral healing, including dealing with difficult or problem ancestors, and why it is so important for us and for our world to learn how to work with our ancestors whoever they may be.

Yvonne Ryves, author of *Shaman Pathways: Web of Life*

Pagan Portals
Ancestral Healing

Edited by Trevor Greenfield

MOON
BOOKS

Winchester, UK
Washington, USA

JOHN HUNT PUBLISHING

First published by Moon Books, 2020
Moon Books is an imprint of John Hunt Publishing Ltd., No. 3 East Street, Alresford
Hampshire SO24 9EE, UK
office@jhpbooks.net
www.johnhuntpublishing.com
www.moon-books.net

For distributor details and how to order please visit the 'Ordering' section on our website.

Text copyright: Trevor Greenfield 2019

ISBN: 978 1 78904 335 8
978 1 78904 336 5 (ebook)
Library of Congress Control Number: 2019948304

A CIP catalogue record for this book is available from the British Library.

Design: Stuart Davies

UK: Printed and bound by CPI Group (UK) Ltd, Croydon, CR0 4YY
US: Printed and bound by Thomson-Shore, 7300 West Joy Road, Dexter, MI 48130

We operate a distinctive and ethical publishing philosophy in
all areas of our business, from our global network of authors to
production and worldwide distribution.

Contents

Healing in the Ancestral Soul

Kenn Day

A full-time working shaman since 1989, I could say a lot about the human soul, ancestor altars, and healing with the ancestors, but the most powerful tool I have ever found for ancestral healing came to me many years after being in practice. Given my considerable work and teaching, I was astounded to discover such an effective, unheard of tool.

In Spring 1998, I took a road trip with my German friend Lisa, a journey detailed in my first book, *Dance of Stones*. We followed a fascinating series of synchronicities to arrive at the Boliegh Fogou, on the grounds of a charming B&B called Rosemerryn House. A few years later, in autumn 2001, Lisa and I returned to Rosemerryn House with a small group of students while on a tour of Cornwall sacred sites. As we all enjoyed a cup of tea together, Lisa told me about Family Constellation Work, a technique in which she was completing her training in Germany. After hearing her description, I asked her if she would be willing to demonstrate the technique.

Lisa had us sit in a circle in the seminar room and then chose one person to be the client. She positioned this person next to her in the circle and asked a few questions about what they might want to change in their life. Then she asked the client to choose a person to represent her mother and one to represent her father and one to represent herself. The client was then to place these representatives intuitively in the space created by our circle. As I watched, I was struck by how easily the client was able to sense where each representative "belonged". Lisa then instructed the client to sit down and to simply watch what occurred. Lisa then entered the field and began to ask the representatives questions about what they were feeling. They responded naturally and

1

easily with information that seemed to be true to the client.

Lisa coaxed the representatives to provide information which led to another person being brought in to represent a child, and then for them to move into a different configuration, which seemed to ease a prior tension evident in the field. As I watched, it was as if I was seeing something deeply familiar but from a completely different perspective. I found myself deeply engaged, both in the constellation in front of me, as well as in my own internal dynamic, as parts of myself began to wake up in response to what I was seeing.

Lisa stepped out of the field and stated that the work was done. The representatives seemed to shake themselves as if they were emerging from a trance.

When another one of my students was chosen as the next client, I settled down to observe more. This time, however, the client chose me to represent his father. I was positioned in the field and instructed to breathe and allow any sensations to arise. I stood there, expectantly awaiting some clear sense of this other person, but it wasn't until Lisa moved next to me and directed my attention at another representative that I realized that I had been completely engrossed in my internal experience and ignoring what was happening around me. I looked at the representative, as instructed, but when asked if I felt anything, all I could report was that I wasn't particularly interested. Lisa then said, would it help if I tell you that this is your son?" Before I could stop myself, I blurted, "Well, that was a mistake!" At this point, the client burst into tears, and I wanted to walk out of the field.

It was finally revealed that the client's father was a narcissist who had been trapped in a brief marriage by the mother's pregnancy. The client reported that everything I had expressed and even the manner in which I had expressed it was uncannily like his estranged father. What struck me as odd was that I had not noticed entering into an altered state or "receiving" any information, and yet, what had come through me was not characteristic of me but the person I was representing.

As I sat and continued to observe, it occurred to me that what I was seeing was the ancestral soul of the client being brought into manifestation through the support of the group. In some mysterious fashion, our circle had allowed the client's ancestral soul not only to show up for all of us but for us to engage it in what seemed to be a meaningful fashion.

Lisa went on to explain that the people working with this technique in Germany had been getting wonderful results, with clients showing tremendous movement on very stubborn issues. What I found exciting though was the notion that this was a way of accessing a huge part of the human experience I had believed I already understood and was working with. And I had been. My work with ancestors and with my own ancestral soul had already helped me to heal considerably from past trauma, but this technique brought the ancestors so much closer than anything I had worked with before.

Family Constellation Work founder Burt Hellinger had first worked as a missionary in South Africa for many years before leaving the church and becoming a therapist. His exposure to ancestor veneration in indigenous populations and his subsequent work with Family Systems Therapy led him to pioneer Constellation Work.

Prior to this initial experience of Constellation Work, I had worked with the ancestors of my clients by Journeying into the Under World and engaging them directly to locate the ancestral source of a client's issue and to ask for their support in addressing it. This often-produced powerful results, but the client, who I would have Journey with me, was often unaware of the interaction and was unable to engage as fully as I would have liked. Constellation Work changed this by bringing the ancestors into the Middle World and making them accessible for the client as well.

After returning from Cornwall, my wife, Patricia, and I

researched training in Constellation Work but found nothing viable in the U.S. at that time. We instead traveled to Germany to visit Lisa, where we attended workshops with the people she knew who were using the work there.

One workshop in Berlin was particularly interesting. When Patricia was the client, she was asked to choose representatives for her six siblings. These were placed in birth order and then allowed to move as they felt appropriate. Each of the representatives clearly expressed the nature of that sibling. The sister who had moved out to California and was very out of touch with the rest of the family moved to the edge of the field and then reported: "I can't get far enough away." The sister who had died recently simply sat down, and we learned that this is often a signal that the person is deceased. In another constellation, I was asked to represent the son of the client. As I entered the field I began staring upward at the ceiling and turning slowly in a circle. I had no sense of the passage of time, but when the facilitator announced that the work was complete, I discovered I had been in this position for some 45 minutes. It was only then that I learned the person I was representing was confined to a mental hospital, and that he spent his days standing and staring at the ceiling, just as I had been. These experiences introduced the deeper realization that the ancestral soul includes not only the deceased but the living as well.

While visiting several other workshops while in Germany, we learned about a two-year certification program offered by Heinz Stark, a Hellinger protégé, that would be presented in Racine, Wisconsin and I decided to enroll.

I was so excited by the first training that Patricia joined me the second week. The two years of training were transformative. When we began the training, I was clear I had no intention of becoming a parent. By the time we were completing training, I was almost as clear that becoming a parent was such a powerful part of the human experience that I was compelled to explore it. Patricia had gone along with me on my initial desire to remain childless, hoping that I would come to my senses. It appears I did. To me, this was a clear indication of the efficacy of Constellation Work as a means of bringing about healing, growth, and transformation at a soul level.

Perhaps the most important thing to note about this practice is that it works. The soul-level movements made by the representatives within the constellation bring about true, **deep**, and lasting changes in the client's life. Further, it is clear that the impact is felt not only in the generations of the living but within the ancestral soul as a whole. The healing reverberations travel back and forth through the generations, often continuing for months after the constellation.

Although Heinz was adamant that we not assume we were actually communicating with the dead, it was clear to me that Constellation Work allowed a window into the client's ancestral soul. Prior to this, I had an understanding of the ancestral soul in much the same way that someone might understand a new dish by reviewing the recipe. After experiencing Constellation Work, I understand the ancestral soul in a much more dynamic way. This has enriched my work with my own ancestors as well as that with my clients and students.

What became apparent to me through this training and my subsequent experience is that when we have a clear relationship with our ancestors, and, when we honor the gift of life which we receive from them, they become a powerful resource in our everyday lives. If there are obstacles to the natural flow of blessings from the ancestors down to us, these blocks can be addressed, in many cases, simply by directing the attention of the ancestors to how their descendants are being harmed by their inattention. The ancestors want their descendants to live well and happily, so they are generally willing to do what they can to support the wellbeing of their offspring. The necessary movement may be as simple as an ancestor acknowledging an aborted child, who is present in the field of the constellation but who was ignored among the living. This is accomplished by speaking to the representative of the ancestor and asking them to acknowledge the child. Once they do so, there is generally a perceptible positive shift in the energetic quality of the field.

There are also cases where the ancestors have become disconnected from their descendants. This can happen when a part of the family emigrates and loses contact with those who remain behind, or when there are many deaths in a short span of time, during a famine, a war, or a disease epidemic.

As we studied and practiced with Heinz, we discovered that Constellation Work allowed access to systems beyond the ancestral soul as well. We found that sometimes individuals appeared in the constellation who were not related by bloodline, but who had become connected to the family line through the taking of a life or the saving of a life. More often, this appeared in one constellation as three representatives who lay down on the floor and reported that they were dead but not related to the family. When we brought in a representative of the great grandfather of the client, he recognized the figures lying on the floor as people of a neighboring village that he had killed and then hidden in a cave. In this case, the solution was to have the other ancestors turn to the victims and bow to them, acknowledging their fate. We thought that this would be enough, but then the great grandfather was drawn to lie down with the victims and when they all lay together, the field eased.

One of the most moving examples of this work was with a client whose family had experienced generations of alcoholism and early death. Her family immigrated to America from Ireland during the famine, and it was apparent that those who had left were no longer connected to their ancestors in the old country. This left them adrift and profoundly hungering for the kind of connection shared by their ancestors. Heinz chose a woman to enter the constellation and stand behind those who had come over. Once she took her place, Heinz said, "I have no idea who this is, but it is clear that those who are here need a strong support, and I felt that something was available here. We will see what happens." As he spoke, the representative seemed to grow taller and more powerful. She seemed larger than life. Heinz move beside her and asked, "How do you feel?" She replied, "I love all of these children. They are all mine." Even her voice was strangely resonant, almost like an organ. Heinz asked her, "Are you their ancestor?" To which she replied, "No. I am Ireland."

The energetic quality of the field broke like a storm in response to this revelation. The representatives burst into tears and turned to face Ireland. Several began speaking without prompting, saying, "I miss you! I am lost without you!" And reporting a deep sense of recognition and reunion. After more than a decade, I am still strongly moved by the memory of that experience. Among other things, it taught me that the Mystery we are working with always reaches beyond our understanding.

When Patricia and I offer a weekend workshop in Constellation Work, the experience is always powerful and moving for all involved. It is very clear that the ancestors, no matter what their actions and attitudes while they were alive, want what is best for us and for all their descendants. At a soul level, all children love their parents and all parents love their children. Furthermore, those who come before us, those who have given the gift of life to us, are always "bigger" than we are, just as we will always carry more spiritual weight than those who come after us. It also becomes clear that the ancestral soul only contains those who share a blood connection with us. It does not include adoptive parents or children, and yet there are connections that allow us to work with these individuals as well.

Some of us have good reasons for not wanting to work with our ancestors, which makes the need for healing all the more apparent. For instance, if we were abused by a member of the family, it is difficult to even want to address the anger and hurt that arises from the experience. I learned a couple of important lessons around this. It is important for the child/client to not forgive the perpetrator. This is at odds with a lot of what is currently assumed to be correct – that healing only comes when we forgive. But what we learned by observing the field of the soul is that it is inappropriate for the child to forgive the adult. When you forgive someone, it tends to place you in a morally superior position to the one you are forgiving, and the soul doesn't like this. It is best to simply tell the adult, "It is not my place to judge you. I am only a child. I leave the consequences of your actions with you. They are not mine to carry." In addition, it can be very helpful to deal with the soul double of the perpetrator, rather than the person they were when they traumatized you. At the soul level, they are more capable of recognizing what they have done and taking responsibility for it in a way they may never be able to do at an ego level.

What is also clear is that, when a good movement happens in the field of the Ancestral Soul during a constellation, that work shows up in all those who share the soul. The work done by one client is shared unconsciously by parents, siblings, and children throughout the family – living and dead. This means that even those who are no longer among the living can – in some cases at least – continue their journey toward growth and healing and that their progress impacts their living descendants as well.

While it is not always possible for clients to attend a workshop, we can also apply the work in private sessions, using stones to represent the ancestors. This still allows direct access to the ancestral soul and those individuals who inhabit the ancestral field. We are then able to engage with these individuals in ways that allow for good movement and healing for the client. Constellation Work also provides a means of extending the more traditional shamanic work with the client and can also work well in conjunction with the client creating an ancestor altar.

Constellation Work IS group shamanism. It directly accesses

the Ancestral Soul in such a way that all those who engage with the field of the soul have an opportunity to experience the nature of this communal sense of Self. Perhaps most importantly, it makes the process much more accessible to the average client, leading to more powerful and effective outcomes. To me, this is what ancestral healing is all about – healing that impacts ourselves, our families and all the ancestors as well.

Kenn Day is a working shaman and the author of *Post-Tribal Shamanism* and *Dance of Stones*.

Walking the Bones: Reconnecting With Our Ancient Past

Taz Thornton

Neglect. That's the word that echoes in my head and heart, time and time again, when I connect to the threads of our past – or, at least, the spirits and energies I find there.

I'm an animist; I believe everything has an energy – a spirit, if you like – and that we can learn endless amounts from the world around us. The rocks, the trees, the land... all have witnessed so much, hold endless wisdom, and yet, it seems the majority of our population, here in the UK, walk around with our eyes – and hearts – closed.

When I think of ancestral healing, this is where I believe the deepest work is needed. We in the western world are at the centre of a head/heart disconnect epidemic. Actually, scratch that – it's worse: head/heart disconnect has become the norm. We've become a culture of heads dragging around bodies – we need to see it to believe it and have everything proven by double blind trials. At the other end of the scale, we blindly follow the preachers, reading from a man-made book, telling us what's right and wrong and keeping us safely in our boxes and under control through fear and doctrine. We've lost connection to the truth of who we are – of who we were, before society told us who it wanted us to be – and we're operating mainly from the neck up. We try to fill the gaps we feel in our soul, the emptiness and listlessness, with materialism. It doesn't work. Keeping up with the Joneses doesn't heal the gaps so many of us are unconsciously aware of – it only creates more gaps in our bank accounts.

We could probably go right back to the coming of the Romans or, perhaps, colonialism, when the powers that be did all they could to wipe out indigenous spirituality and force everyone under control of The Church (sorry – save everyone and convert them to Christianity), but we're way beyond finger pointing having any real value. What's important now is to find a way to reconnect us all to the lands on which we walk, the teachings and knowledge we left behind. We need to reconnect to that heart that beats deep within Mother Earth – the one that connects us all.

We need only to look around at the surge in popularity of self-help books in recent years, at the numbers of 'life coaches' we see today, the emphasis on journaling, mindfulness and meditation. A glimpse at the mind, body, spirit section of even the most mainstream bookshop will present to us sets of oracle cards based on everything from unicorns and cats to trees and past lives. People are searching for something more. We might not know what we're looking for, but we're desperately scrabbling around to connect to something. Anything. Surely, there must be more than this?

Back to materialism – or, at least, capitalism (with a soft 'c') – that pull within us, that call to discover the meaning of life, the universe and everything beyond, that longing to feel something more is at least creating a boon for the mind, body, spirit 'industry' – the sector seems to be growing faster than ever before. There's nothing wrong with that. Hey, for the record, I'm part of it – I run workshops and retreats, I coach people one-to-one and in groups, I help guide people who feel 'lost' or, more to the point, I help them to get back in touch with the truth of who they are and discover how to guide themselves into the future in a more balanced way.

I'm writing this not to bash therapists, healers, coaches, authors – all those who make a living through helping and supporting others. In fact, the opposite is true: we need good people who are skilled in rebalancing energies and steering questers through the quagmire society has created more than ever. I tire of people criticising those who charge fees for their healing work – wherever we argue that spirit/energy comes from, they've still invested the time and money into training and honing their abilities and they're still using their time to support those in need; if we want these people to be available to help us, we need to respect their needs and boundaries as well – they have bills and mortgages like everyone else and they're offering a professional service.

I mention the amount of people who are now in the business of serving others simply as another indicator of where we have ended up as a people. Professions and industries spring up and thrive in a response to need. Our society has created a need for more professional healers, coaches, therapists, more self-help books, more sets of oracle cards, more reading materials and information on every branch of spirituality you can think of – and then some.

We are a society of seekers – and it's my belief that we're being driven by a deep realisation that somewhere along the way, we lost something. We let something go. We allowed fast cars, designer watches, consumerism and the media popularity contest to erode our connection to all that is. We created head/heart disconnect. I find this in so many of the people I work with in my capacity as a coach, and with those who join my spiritual empowerment programmes. Many people have lost their sense of identity and connection; beyond being a mum, a father, a business owner, a manager in a corporate chain, they don't actually know who they are, why they're here or where they belong – sometimes, even, if they belong.

Our sense of identity has lost dimension and we need to get it back. That, for me, comes with slowing down, learning to quieten the monkey mind, tuning back into our senses, reattuning with all that is. Perhaps it begins with meditation or, maybe, getting away from the office blocks and modern coffee shops with those perfect blends, and into nature. When was the last time you walked barefoot on the earth? When was the last time you sat down in a meadow without worrying about getting grass stains on your designer jeans? When was the last time you left your watch at home and allowed your senses, the temperature and the light to guide your day? When did you last actually look at a tree, rather than blindly moving past a hunk of wood? Have you spent time just being in the presence of that tree, sensing the age, wondering how much it might have been witness to, marvelling at the slowness of growth, the strength, the deep, deep roots?

When I was learning about the medicine path, I will always remember one of my teachers, Chris Lüttuchau, talking about Starchild energy. There's a whole raft of really power-full teachings about archetypes – I use them a lot in my work – and one of those archetypes is the Starchild; it's the element of ourselves that still sees the magic and wonder in all things. All too often, I find people have lost connection to that sense of awe.

Years ago, when I was still in the corporate world, I was on a road trip with my assistant. We ended up on a stretch of road somewhere near Buckinghamshire and I remember looking up and seeing the skies filled with red kites – it was when their reintroduction was still in its infancy compared to today, where these magnificent birds of prey are now commonplace in some parts of the UK. I was mesmerised – I counted a dozen of them, all circling, catching the thermals in an amazing overhead display. "Oh wow!" I remember saying, "Look at that – red kites – they're one of our largest birds of prey – aren't they magnificent?!" My assistant looked at me as if I was totally crazy and shrugged: "What? It's just a bird." This wonderful woman, both friend and colleague, just couldn't grasp why I would think something so beautiful, so out of the ordinary, so utterly part of the natural world, was anything to be excited about.

For me, we were being gifted with something magical, whilst

travelling in traffic, on a road that seemed to be going on forever. The stress of the journey lifted and that starchild energy kept flooding in. For her, we'd been driving for ages, she wanted to get home, and I was making a ridiculously big deal out of a few random birds; they might as well have been pigeons (which, of course, are also beautiful and full of teachings, if far more commonplace).

That might seem like a strange story to share as part of this book but, for me, it illustrates a small element of what we've lost. If we can really go through life being aware of nothing but the man-made 'stuff' around us or, at least, not acknowledging the wonders of nature, it's no wonder so many of us are feeling lack. And that brings me right back to the word I began this chapter with: neglect. We're neglecting to notice, and to connect with, the world around us. We've stopped noticing the small, everyday miracles. We're looking, but we're not seeing.

Don't get me wrong, I can appreciate finely crafted clothes, jewellery, bags, cars and shoes as much as the next person. I can even enjoy the odd day in a shopping centre. But there's more to life than that; we need more to truly fill us up, from the inside out.

We need the sunlight.
We need the trees.
We need the stars.
We need fresh air.
We need to connect to the spirit and energy of all our relations.

When I wrote my first book, *Whispers From The Earth*, I spent a long time connecting to the energies of places, meditating, doing journey work, in an attempt to find some link with our ancestral pasts – the threads of those who walked these lands long, long before we were ever born. The result was an anthology of channelled teaching stories but, those aside, I felt a deep longing from those old, old, energies to be acknowledged and worked with.

This earth of ours holds the bones, the teeth and the blood of the ancestors and yet, so often, we neglect to connect with that deep, ancient wisdom. All too often, when people start to notice that head/heart disconnect, when they begin to realise that something is missing in their life and want to quest for something more, they start to explore spiritual paths. This, sometimes, is where our learned, ingrained materialism and lack of awareness of the world around us leads us away from the magic right beneath our feet, above us and in every direction.

People's quests to reconnect with something more, something greater, something special and exotic, take them to far flung places. The great pyramids of Egypt. Australia. New Zealand. The Amazon. Easter Island. New Mexico. America. China. It's easy to understand why people might grasp for the bright, shiny threads of accessible spiritual pathways, available at the swipe of a credit card and at the end of a long flight, though I can't help but feel we're missing something really important. Sure, explore, globetrot, experience new places, but please, please, if you're looking to fill your heart and soul, start where you are.

The British Isles are full of beautiful, wonderful spirituality. Yes, the trails are sometimes harder to pick up. Yes, much of our indigenous spirituality was rubbed out by those who came before us who, however misguided it might seem now, believed they were doing the right thing. Yes, it's ridiculously hard to find much solid information to go on pre-Roman invasion. And yet, these lands are full of beautiful, magical healing energy and wonderful teachings, if only we're willing to tune in and search for them.

I love visiting our ancient sites – not just Stone Henge and the tourist havens, but those a little off the beaten track that only a committed enthusiast might find. They might not have cafes and tourist shops, you might not be able to take home an image of that hill fort, barrow or stone circle on a tea towel or buy a commemorative pen, but the energies are great.

That said, you can tap into the wonders of our ancient past pretty much wherever you go. Whether you're walking an ancient woodland or strolling between new saplings, exploring Avebury or walking across tiny pebbles on the beach, go deep enough and the ground on which you walk will hold you, guide you and, sometimes, even heal you.

If you follow a spiritual path that allows you to safely, and sanely, connect with the spirits of the place, you might even be able to pick up that whisper on the breeze that tells great stories or offers advice along your path – that's one kind of life coaching you don't need to pay for, though it can be polite to at least leave some kind of offering (whilst not littering and ensuring you're leaving every place you tread more beautiful than you found it, of course).

And it's not just places. The elements are around us at all times. The spirits of earth, fire, air and water are there for us to connect to whenever we choose. Energy and spirit are everywhere. If you reach a point in your life where you realise there's something missing and you need to discover something more, you really can start wherever you happen to be. Breathe in. Breathe out. Breathe in. Breathe out. Ground yourself. Feel the earth beneath your feet, feel the air you pull into your lungs, feel the sunlight (or rain) on your brow, feel the powers of the four directions all around you.

We are never alone. When we start to reconnect, when we start to undo that block between our head and our heart, when we start to build our awareness, to open ourselves up, to move into that expansive place where we begin to really notice and come alive, we are home. Whilst walking around Stanton Drew stone circle, in Somerset, I felt drawn to one of the stones that looked to have been damaged. Using the shamanic techniques

16

I work with, I connected with the stone and asked if it had any wisdom to share. Teachings and medicine really are all around us. Here's what came:

Words From A Broken Stone

Sometimes we break. Are we not still strong? Do we not still hold our ground, standing tall in the mightiest winds, the heaviest rains? Does Grandfather Sun not cast his light upon us? Strength, little one, is not to be impervious to breaks; strength is to stand witness, to endure, to crack when circumstances beyond our control require that of us – when WE can withstand no more.

When we break, we know that the Great Mother will always catch us and soften our fall; strength is in allowing, trusting, knowing. Strength is sometimes to be found within the cracks that form. When we allow the Grandfather's rays to spill into our wounds, to fill us with warmth. When we learn and grow and come to love – and respect – our new shape. It is not our height that allows us to stand tall – it is our presence, our wisdom, our knowledge, our courage.

We stand here, surrounded by grasses and trees. When the great wind blows, they bend and sway; they dance as the pressure builds and, so, remain unscathed. We cannot dance. We cannot sway. We cannot move with the storms or lean into the breeze as the great winds blow. And so, in our rigidity, sometimes, we break. And we learn and we grow. And we stand strong through our tumultuous adventures.

Strength is not to be found in those who never break, little one. Strength is in those who allow themselves to fall, knowing they will be caught, trusting they will be held and loving the warrior they will become. Go. Be strong. Have faith. Know that we will be here, through the strongest of gales, the heaviest of rains, the most thunderous of storms, the coldest of winters and the balmiest of summers. We will

17

endure. We will learn. We will deepen our wisdom. We will grow. As will you.

Taz Thornton is a shamanic healer, crafter and workshop leader, firewalker and empowerment coach, reiki master and writer. She is the author of *Whispers from the Earth*.

Intergenerational Silence: Witnessing Yesterday to Heal Today

Irisanya Moon

Anything that's human is mentionable, and anything that is mentionable can be more manageable. When we can talk about our feelings, they become less overwhelming, less upsetting, and less scary. The people we trust with that important talk can help us know that we are not alone. — Fred Rogers

When things hurt, when things are hard, we often turn inwards. We turn into ourselves, we turn into the places of confusion and self-doubt, thinking that if we look hard enough, we'll see that it was our fault – and thus, our responsibility to figure things out. We look to others in our lives and we see stories of 'they never complained' or 'they never said a thing.' And for some reason, we celebrate this as a strength. We compliment it, even aspire to it. We emulate it. We become alone in our worry, alone in our traumas, and alone in our healing.

When Trauma Happens

Trauma is often thought of as the worst thing that could ever happen to a person ever. A shooting. A devastating accident. A life-changing illness. War. Abuse.

Society often confines trauma to a situation that was so horrible that it is clear how damaging it is. Anyone would be traumatized after being hurt or watching someone be hurt or being in a place where safety was conditional – and not reliable. Even Merriam-Webster notes that trauma is:

a very difficult or unpleasant experience that causes someone to have mental or emotional problems usually for a long time.

This definition makes trauma a little wider and broader. It opens up the possibility that trauma is in the eye of the one who experiences it, versus being limited to what another defines trauma to be. Trauma interrupts what is known. It enters into what is expected, changes the presumed reality, and causes questioning of all that comes after.

It happens and we don't know what to do. Our brains are ignited. Our fight, flight, or freeze response is activated. Our animal selves know that we could fight what is happening (but that doesn't necessarily work or have a place in some trauma situations). We could flee the situation (but that isn't always possible as we need to deal with the outcomes, the ramifications).

Or we could freeze. We could stay still enough so as not to be noticed or hurt any further. We could freeze until things feel safe again. But they don't always feel safe again, not with the memory of what has happened.

The Entrance of Silence

I remember watching my parents deal with big life events. Something disastrous would happen and they would say as little as possible. They would never talk about it after the initial announcement. They seemed to have no feelings or few feelings. And while it's true I don't know what happened when I wasn't around, the overwhelming message I received was 'time will heal things.' 'You just need to wait it out.' 'Don't talk about it because that just brings up all the bad feelings again.' If you talk about it, you'll just relive it. And no one wants that.

The events, the feelings would come out in other ways. Anger. Depression. Hostility. All of the feelings that were 'bad' were suppressed until they could not be contained. And then the person who finally let them free would be seen as dangerous or unbalanced. The feelings were stuffed back again. My parents learned this from their parents, stoic German people. Work, because that's what gets you ahead. Move on because you have other things to do.

People who were emotional were weak, I was taught in the silence. People who let things 'get to them' were somehow damaged. They were 'bad' people. After all, they expressed feelings that were hard to contain. They said things that were hurtful. They clearly didn't care about others because of this self-serving release of emotions. Instead, be quiet. Eventually, you will feel better. But the truth is that all of these messages led to internalized feelings of being a bad person if I ever had a feeling that wasn't acceptable in society. These messages led to more silence and more repression. They led to unhealthy ways of coping, strained relationships, and the ever-present feeling of being unable to be just as I was. Sad. Angry. Not okay.

When the Unexpected Happened

In the years after an abusive relationship, I never said anything about the rape that I thought wasn't rape. After all, I didn't say no, but I also didn't consent. I kept my feelings and my anger to myself. I let it fester in my mind as clearly something I had done wrong. When my bosses would touch me or make crude remarks, I learned to keep quiet. And in the moments when I didn't hold my tongue, I was reprimanded for causing trouble, for not being a team player.

After my mom was killed in a car accident, I remember the overwhelming feelings that rose from my heart into my head. I remember the way I didn't know what to feel or how to feel it or what to do when everything crashed – literally and figuratively. I stood in my backyard after the phone call and tried to bring my mind into the present moment.

But my mind wanted nothing to do with what was happening. It wanted to hide. It wanted to curl up into a little ball. It wanted to say nothing because if I said nothing, perhaps it wouldn't be real.

I watched my heart build up walls. I watched myself pull away and isolate. I knew better too. I knew that talking was the way to healing. I tried to find ways to talk, to express, and to build connections through my vulnerability. I really tried. But in a world that wants everything to be easy and comfortable, I found myself feeling more and more alone.

I would talk to my dad about my mom, only to hear him get upset and angry. These are completely normal emotions and these emotions need to move through the body to become softened. But I wanted my dad to be okay. I noticed how when I didn't bring something up or try to talk about my mom, he would be steady.

I tried to talk to my siblings about my mom, only to hear that they were fine, just fine. But I also knew that they were angrier than they were before her death. I also knew they were sad in private, but rarely in public after the funeral. Silently, we suffered when we could have come together.

It's the same with other traumas. I know of many people who have been raped and assaulted. But I only know these stories because at one point, they came into a conversation. Often, in the safety of ritual or sacred circles, we didn't worry about being quiet anymore. We didn't worry about upsetting or revealing that the world has hurt us so badly that our bones are heavy with loss.

However, sometimes, those stories went right back into the shadows. We never talked about them again. It's not necessarily our fault that we cling to silence. It does seem to be the action that is the easiest road, the most acceptable way to relate. We believe that we will burden others when we say what we really feel. But we are also hiding things and showing others that hiding is the thing to do.

What if we could do better? What if we could resist the overculture's need to keep us quiet and compliant? What if we could speak up and speak loudly so others would feel permission to do the same? What if we could live in a world that doesn't encourage a stiff upper lip? What if we could live in a world that normalized trauma and offered safe, soft places to be just as we are?

The Weight of Untold Stories

The stories we carry are often the stories we become. Their weight, their sharpness can infuse us and infect us. Whether you name this as trauma or not, there are generations of people who are weighed down by what they have been asked to bear on their own.

In the moments that follow, in the years that follow, the wake of trauma's damage becomes apparent.

Anxiety
Panic
Post-Traumatic Stress Disorder (PTSD)
Insomnia
Nightmares
Fear of _____
Dissociation

The physical symptoms of held-back feelings came as headaches, stomach issues, tense muscles, erratic eating habits, chest tightness, and a sense that I would never be safe again.

We will often feel 'off' on a day that looks or feels like the day the trauma happened. We might be unsettled by the way the light falls into a window or the way the room smells. On the actual anniversary of the event, we might crumble or lash out.

Our bodies remember. Our minds remember. And even when we don't say a thing, the stories are there. They lie in wait to be known. They patiently settle into our cells because they're not going anywhere. They're a part of us. But you can't hold back the ocean with a thin wall of avoidance.

Magick and Healing and the Telling of Stories

I remember the first time I told the story of rape. I was in a room with witches and we were sharing our hearts in sacred space. Throughout my sharing, I watched myself say things I had never said aloud. I watched myself, as though I were a movie, speak things that were true and honest and raw. After all, this was their first time in the light.

That's not completely true. I told my story in poetry in which I made the speaker someone who was not myself. I said it was fiction, a made-up tale about a person I knew. I said I wanted to speak for those who didn't have a voice. But I was speaking for myself. And in the dismissal of my own voice, I felt I was betraying my core being. Again.

And all throughout that time, I felt ill. I felt like I was a person who should have dealt with this by now. It had been years. I should have known better. I should have said no. I should have broken up with this person. I should have been stronger. I watched myself list off the reasons why I was silent all those years.

It took a friend who had a similar experience to tell me that I didn't deserve any of those things. None of what happened was my fault. I was not alone. That was the moment of spilling over, of releasing the ocean. In that ocean was grief and anger and awareness. In that ocean were tears that I had never shed. In that ocean were waves that crashed against everything. Those crashing waves smoothed me, over and over, until the rocks that weighed my down were smooth pebbles. Lighter.

Stopping the Silence

Stopping the cycle of silence begins with a word, then another word, and then another word. It begins when you fight against what you thought was the 'right' way to do things and you start heading onto the uncomfortable path of healing.

Tell anyone – Find a friend, a tree, a stone, or a god and talk to them. Tell them the story of your pain, your anger, and your sadness. Tell them the story just as it was, without apology or explanation. Ask that they hold you as a witness, not a problem solver. Ask that they receive this story as an offering of vulnerability.

Remind yourself of your worth – It is easy in trauma to find ways to blame yourself. Whether you blame yourself for being assaulted or you blame yourself for not being the best _____ to someone before they died, take a breath and come back to your core self. If you need to make a list of all of the things that are wonderful about you, do that. If you need to stand in a mirror and say, "I love you" until you believe it, do that. Remind yourself that your stories are valuable, that your silence does not serve anyone, especially yourself.

Writing / Art / Song – The more you can bring your story out into the light, the less you will turn to silence. You are never alone in your wandering through trauma. Not everyone will understand, but someone will. Maybe you share your creation or maybe you just share it with yourself. The more you tell the story (or stories), the easier it becomes to break the cycle.

Devote yourself – It can help to find a deity that can hold you or protect you. This might look like a fierce warrior who protects you from harm. It might look like a soothing energy that can wipe away your tears. It might be a deity who simply sits with you and listens. Find a spiritual guide and show up to be with them – and allow them to be with you too.

Gratitude – In silence, the vacuum created often sucks in negative thoughts. And this is normal and to be expected, though not always helpful or healing. Instead of promising yourself to be positive all the time, begin a practice of gratitude that enables you to remember what IS good right now. I am grateful that I am safe. I am grateful that my body is my own. I am grateful for my heart that is healing.

Mental health professionals – To be clear, when trauma

and the surrounding silence is too much and you find yourself unable (or unwilling) to move in another direction, therapy with a trained mental health professional is ideal. You can find cost-conscious resources in most areas, and there are also online resources to talk to someone.

What you're cultivating with these practices is the ability to say what needs to be said. You will learn that not everyone can hold what you have to offer, but you will find those who can. In fact, you might be surprised to hear that your opening encourages others to say the words they've also held back.

A Ritual for Healing Across the Generations

You can do the work for yourself, but the trauma that's carried settles in your body. And you may also carry trauma from previous generations in unspoken words and learned behaviors.

You may want to do a ritual to help heal all of the generations who were silence, while also offering healing to the future generations so they might unburden themselves when they find themselves in similar situations.

If you can, find pictures of relatives and ancestors who encouraged your silence. You might use these pictures on an altar, photocopy pictures to add to a collage, or decorate a candle with their names. Simply create a focal point where they can be so you can direct your attention and intention to them.

When you have found a place for them to be, create a sacred space where you will not be disturbed. Ground yourself, cast a circle, call in the elements, and call on your allies to aid your work. Tell your stories to your ancestors. Tell them all of the things you need to say and allow yourself to feel heard. Allow yourself to have the emotions that come up, without judging them. Just be in the moment and break the silence.

It might be helpful at this point to offer forgiveness to those who taught you to be silent. They may very well have believed they were protecting you from hurt. They may have only learned this from previous generations. If it feels right, forgive them.

If you find yourself with complicated relatives and silence that was forced upon you as a tool of control, you might find it supportive to let the past generations know that you will not be silent anymore. Repeat three times:

I am breaking the cycle of silence.
I am breaking the cycle of silence.
I am breaking the cycle of silence.

Whatever you decide to do, allow yourself to sit in the new silence that emerges. It might come with an emotional release. It might come with whispers of wisdom. It might settle in your bones as newfound energy or as deep relief. You might find the energy moves from the past to the present and into the future.

Stay in the sacred space until you feel ready to release your sacred space. Extinguish the candle with a snuffer or your finger tip. Repeat as you need. Remember, your release of silence is a healing act. It is an act of empowerment and courage. You are not alone, you never were.

Irisanya Moon is a Witch, Reclaiming initiate, priestess, teacher, and writer. She is the author of *Reclaiming Witchcraft* and *Aphrodite*.

Of Things Lost and Love Gained

Imelda Almqvist

The Bones hold the Essence and the Stones hold the Memories
Wisdom from the Mystical Hebrew Teachings, Richard Lenson

What happens to stories no one tells any longer and what is the fate of forgotten gods? Is there a clearing in the forest where they have a secret hut and gather? Do they stalk the dreams of humans in the hope of being heard or seen? Do they shape shift into birds and peck on the windows of our soul? As a forest witch, I love finding bones and skulls. They all have a story to tell and they sing at night. They sculpt my dreams and transport my soul. Recently I was flying from Stockholm to London with some deer bones in my hand luggage (for a TV program). "Are those human bones?" I was asked at security. "No Sir, deer bones!" That's fine then, Madam – enjoy your flight!

Something needs to be covered before it can be recovered or uncovered. Finding physical bones always makes me whether our ancestors buried any metaphoric bones. Those wise men and women, the wisdom keepers, who knew how to navigate both cosmos and human psyche, faced an impossible situation when cataclysms and paradigm shifts occurred. Not only were their own lives in danger, but the wisdom of our deep ancestors (those whose names we do not remember) was teetering on the edge of an abyss called oblivion.

What does one do in times of great moral peril? Just possibly one covers things and hides them, in plain sight, in the forest, under a coat of Christian varnish, in myths and nursery rhymes, planted in the ear of a willing child or inside hollow bones. Perhaps one day someone will uncover the material, so the voices of the ancestors reach their descendants across the mists of time?

Someone I know started shamanic training and the spirits gave her song. When she sang that song to her family (in her fatherland and mother tongue) she was told: "That is the song your grandfather used to sing!" The song had returned after many decades of being lost. We hurt ourselves when we lose touch with our ancestors. It is a form of spiritual amputation. We become rootless trees and topple easily; the phantom limbs haunt us. We also hurt our ancestors – they deserve better. Most of all ancestors wish to be remembered. We ourselves are the ancestors of future generations! What are pain and trauma, really? What purpose do they serve?

Pain is a universal experience that serves the vital function of triggering avoidance. The pain sensation is a necessary part of being human. Pain sensation is a fact of life
https://www.sharecare.com/health/pain-management/what-is-purpose-of-pain

Pain is a hard taskmaster. Human beings spend a lot of time and effort avoiding pain. From small pains toddlers learn to avoid bigger pains or life-threatening scenarios. From broken hearts adult humans learn about discernment, healthy boundaries and not giving their soul away. Having acknowledged that, pain is not only about "triggering avoidance". There is more to it:

Pain often is something coming to attention because it seeks healing! Human beings try to avoid pain, but it always catches up (sooner or later). Sometimes it catches up at a considerable delay, meaning that unresolved issues will surface again in the descendants of people long dead.

Pain does not evaporate when a person dies. It is either healed (transmuted, balanced and any wrongdoing forgiven) or, if not, it pools in the ancestral field. Someone, one day, *must* carry it again – *because it needs healing and working through.* In mysterious ways certain types of pain are *impersonal.* We often carry the pain of people we never met. The pain of our ancestors lives on in our bodies. Their terror lives on in our nightmares.

When we engage with deep-rooted pain in meaningful ways we nearly always find ancestral pain too. We entered a layered landscape that interacts with both dreams and mythology (C.J. Jung called this The Collective Unconscious). Through healing my own pain, I understand the pain of my parents, my forefathers and foremothers. I gain precious insights into the forces and limitations that shaped their lives: the abuse that was passed on, the wars they lived through, the children they lost, the medical care they did not receive.

Not only that, I gain the opportunity to heal some of these things. I can offer apologies where an apology is due. I can ask healing spirits to unravel and transmute unhealthy entanglements. I can make amends for things my ancestors did. If I do not undertake this work – who will?!

Because all families are riddled with trauma and ancestral grief (as well as wonderful memories, great achievements and super cool genes) we are *all* affected by this phenomenon. Most of us do not realise this or consciously work with this. Some people do not realise that they are living an ancestral dream – rather than dreaming their own authentic dream. They become the medical doctor their grandfather had wanted to be rather than the pop musician their soul craves to be.

Traumatised people often traumatise others in turn. What this really means is "making others carry our pain for a while" because it brings the illusion of relief, of having shifted it. However, this sensation is short-lived. Only too soon, pain and trauma will be singing in our blood, bones and dreams again. And not only that: there is now another person who carries this trauma. *Trauma breeds and spreads – when it goes unchecked.* This is one the most powerful motivations for engaging in ancestral healing work! Healing, balancing and transmuting such imprints, memories and issues can clear the family line. We free future generations from being affected and burdened by this. By clearing ourselves we also reduce the chance of us inadvertently hurting (or even traumatising!) those around us. Those are major gains, in a culture where mental illness has reached epidemic proportions. *There are things we human beings want to eradicate – but can't. There are also things we desperately want to retrieve – but can't.*

In the past desperate attempts have been made to stamp out certain things for once and for all. Witchcraft is one obvious example. Old Europe was profoundly Heathen. When Christianity started spreading, the church fathers believed that many ancient practices could be eliminated, and they took draconic measures to achieve this. The old gods became "demons" and Satan arrived on the scene.

Medicine plants had the names of saints forced on them and even star constellations (named groups of stars not on the zodiac are called asterisms) did not get off scot-free. Lady Bedstraw (*galium verum*) used to be called *Friggjargras* in Old Norse (the grass of the goddess Frigg). The three-star asterism that we call Orion's Belt today was known as *Frigg's distaff* to the Early Scandinavian peoples. It is situated on the celestial equator and it is possible that the rotation of the night sky (which visibly spins like a great wheel around the pole star, if you stay out all night and watch the stars for long enough) reminded our Northern European ancestors of Frigg's spinning wheel. The Old Norse name for the planet Venus was *Friggjarstjarna*, Frigg's star.

I believe that the zero-tolerance stance on "nature worship" (consciously living in harmony and reciprocity with the in-dwelling spirits of natural phenomena, animals and features in the landscape) is one taproot of the ecological crisis we face today. We see a proliferation of workshops where people learn to hug trees, communicate with animals and assemble a home pharmacy of natural remedies. This is one reaction to the great "stamping out". The philosopher Hegel called this process *dialectic swing*: things first swing to one extreme and then to another, before any balance over middle ground can be found. (However, the middle ground is only a starting point – another dialectic swing soon starts and this is how human consciousness evolves).

Often the early conversions were only skin-deep, especially in the rural areas, where wise men and cunning women continued to practice what they had always done: healing, herbalism, midwifery, divination work, speaking to the dead and helping lost souls cross over. Another wave of "total eradication" occurred in the form of the witch hunts of the late sixteenth and early seventeenth centuries. Twentieth century Europe brought the Holocaust where, once again, the prevailing doctrine was that there could be a "final solution" and "total elimination" of certain groups in society. A very large group of people alive today carries the horror and ancestral impact of this in their souls and bones.

The Norse cosmology that is so close to my heart was appropriated by Nazi ideology and abused – this issue still requires on-going healing and re-education: wiping perceived stains off the heritage. Much scholarship has been done on the Norse myths which remain to us. The core texts are the *Poetic Edda* and the *Prose Edda*. Debates rage. Some scholars claim that the core texts are truly ancient and that they give us the blueprints of old pagan rituals, beliefs and mysteries. Other scholars remain convinced that because those texts were written down after Christianity became the dominant religion in Europe, (there was only oral transmission in earlier times), we are seeing Christian themes wearing a "pagan coat" (Odin hanging on the world tree is then perceived as a pagan version of the crucifixion of Christ. However, Odin was around long before Christ was born and archaeological finds show that initiation practices involving ceremonial hanging and trees existed in Stone Age Scandinavia). Icelandic historian, poet and politician Snorri Sturluson, who gave us The Prose Edda, definitely showed a Christian bias in his vivid descriptions.

However, thanks to Snorri we have access to texts and information that would have been lost otherwise. I greatly appreciate all scholarship done in Old Norse and Early Scandinavian studies but first and last, I am a practitioner of the material – not an academic. I learn most from *direct interaction* with the worlds and spirits of this cosmology. It does not matter whether we call this "shamanic journeying" or "UPG – Unique Personal Gnosis". Academics will never consider this direct dialogue an acceptable source of information and many practitioners will always feel that academics often miss the point because they are not believers. Even Christianity teaches that faith alone can truly unlock the key mysteries. One definition of a sacrament is a visible sign of an inward grace. My essay does not even attempt to close the chasm between scholarship and religious experience.

Once we open ourselves to any spiritual process of direct information gathering, many doors open and we find clues and divine guidance hidden everywhere. Those doors can obviously not open for people who do not believe in those doors. I believe that the Norse gods are powerful enough to communicate with me using all modern means available to them (and me) Many people will disagree with me. What is clear is that we cannot go live in Viking Age Scandinavia again – *we must work with what we have.*

This essay explores how (and whether) something vibrant can be eliminated and gone forever. Unintentionally, humans have achieved this in terms of the frightening acceleration of animal species going extinct. The dinosaurs became extinct without human intervention. The sheer number and life-style of human beings today (over-population, global warming) are pushing many animal species into extinction.

It is also an undeniable fact that certain dialectic swings have always occurred. Just as cultures have always been encountered and invaded by other cultures introducing new deities, a new cosmology and new rules of engagement. The higher octave manifestation of this is cross-fertilisation and fruitful cultural exchange (and often a larger pantheon). The lower octave manifestation of this is warfare and genocide.

Just as we live in times of great change, others did before us. And just as many of us wonder where we are headed (collectively speaking) elders of ancient communities must have done so before us. If you had reliable inside information that your culture stood little chance of surviving some imminent onslaught or cataclysm – what would you do? Perhaps you would try to hide clues and snippets of key information in places where no one of the current dominant mindset would look for them. You could call this "hiding things in plain sight". Songs we sing to children are one example of this. A Swedish herbalist once told me that a certain Swedish nursery rhyme (ironically belted out by many generations of young children in nursery school) is really an abortifacient recipe: it tells you what herbs to use to make the mixture – and where to find them.

Stories can be like hollow bones: the surface story may give little indication of the deeper darker truths that hide right under the bright colours and childish details. Some scholars are engaged in innovative work decoding hidden messages in fairy tales and children's rhymes. Academic and folklorist Jack Zipes convincingly showed how fairy tales can be used to shape or destabilize attitudes and behaviour within culture. They...

serve a meaningful social function, not just for compensation but for revelation: the worlds projected by the best of our fairy tales reveal the gaps between truth and falsehood in our immediate society. (https://en.wikipedia.org/wiki/Jack_Zipes)

Anthropologists Marcel Griaule and Germaine Dieterlen, in the 1930s, 40s and 50s, claimed to have found evidence of advanced modern astronomical knowledge, such as comprehension of the binary nature of star system Sirius and Saturn's rings, which can only be seen using a telescope, in the religious teachings of a 20th century Stone Age tribe (The Dogon people in Mali, West Africa).

Professional opinion stands divided here too. Some authors and experts believe that this type of research can bring great revelations and additions to our current knowledge base. Other authors believe that we will always find evidence for whatever we choose to believe in the first place and therefore the argument is "circular". Psychologists call this the Confirmation Bias: the tendency to search for, interpret, favour, and recall information in a way that confirms one's pre-existing beliefs or hypotheses.

This is another riddle I am not going to solve in this essay! What I *will* say is that our ancestral field demonstrates just how a *knowing field* (the term was coined by Bert Hellinger who gave us family constellations work) holds memories and deep knowledge without any specific person or organisation acting as the Cosmic Librarian or Chief Archivist. Those memories and imprints can be accessed quite easily used shamanic or related means. Seen from that perspective "The Human Family" is one huge organism whose memories remain as cellular imprints.

Research now shows that ancestral experiences become encoded or stored in our DNA, this is called *genetic memory*. So here we have another mysterious yet powerful knowledge base. (https://www.vice.com/en_au/article/ypv58j/genetic-memory) My colleague Richard Lenson, (a retired bone surgeon), explains that a bone is the container for bone marrow. This marrow, in an embryo, contains pluripotent cells which have the ability to develop into many different types of biological tissue. These cells are encased in the cavity of our bones.

Marrying two phenomena: the human inability to eliminate

unwanted things and deep desire to retrieve lost-but-wanted things, I suggest that we have not exhausted all possibilities yet. If we are willing to open ourselves to a wider scope of perceiving reality (and using ancient techniques that produce meaningful results, even if those are "non-scientific" or "non-academic" by contemporary Western standards) then both immense healing and profound learning can occur. *Hearing ancestral voices again brings both personal and intergenerational healing. Calling excluded souls back to the family fold benefits all descendants and restores harmony.*

This work demands fearless self-examination, unconditional inclusion of everyone who belongs to our tribe, apology work, the unravelling of curses and extraction of ghosts. *What am I hearing or seeing behind the surface information? What is not being said? What do the loudest silences convey?!*

Behind a saint, or the (Christian) Mother of God we find ancient Germanic goddesses. Behind those goddesses we find even an even older presence or mystery, a Neolithic bird goddess or Paleolithic Sun Goddess (who remains visible today in the abundant rock art of Scandinavia). The Sun is a circle. The Moon is a circle. The Earth is a circle. Their mysteries and secrets are circular – not linear. Once we open our senses and widen our perception, we can enter those circles at any point on the "wheel" (the runes are such points on the cosmic wheel.) The night sky continues to spin above us – even when light pollution hides this spectacle from many city dwellers.

One teaching from physics is that energy cannot be destroyed – it can only change form, or (in shamanic parlance) "shape shift into something else". Nothing is ever utterly and completely lost; things move into a parallel dimension. That is what Death is – an energetic shift, what physicists call "a phase transition". In shamanism we call this *stepping outside time*. Outside Time, nothing is truly lost. All that ever was (Is, or Will Be) exists in energetic form, as a vibration or frequency. It can be accessed in altered states of consciousness. We can visit the deceased or great cosmic libraries in other worlds – much can be retrieved. On that level, oblivion is an illusion – but this can *never ever* justify extermination or avoidable extinction of any sentient beings!

Sadly, most of us have lost our library ticket: the deep inner knowing that navigating other worlds is our birth right and that we all do this at night, in our dreams. In these realms our ancestors can be consulted and extinct animal species encountered. There is far more to be uncovered as the human capacity to understand expands.

Imelda Almqvist is a shamanic teacher and painter. She teaches courses in shamanism and sacred art internationally and her paintings appear in art collections all over the world. She is the author of *Natural Born Shamans* and *Sacred Art - A Hollow Bone for Spirit.*

Dealing with Ancestral Shame

Mabh Savage

Honouring the ancestors is an integral part of many pagan paths. Heathenry, Wicca, some Celtic based paths and many others all include ancestral veneration. This is the acknowledgment and gratitude towards people who came before them, either as direct ancestors or as people who had significance either in their lives, their communities, or upon the path that they follow. The idea being that without their ancestors, people would not be who they are, or where they are today. This makes perfect sense. We are each the culmination of generations up generations of genetic material, plus our upbringing is an intricate tapestry of what our parents learned from their grandparents, and so on, going back for thousands of years.

Honouring the ancestors is fine when you are proud of your ancestors. It can lend substance and richness to spirituality, and create a firm foundation for a deeper understanding of self. But when you have ancestors that have done things that make you uncomfortable, it becomes problematic. Why should you honour someone who you would not choose to be friends with today? Who you might actively stay away from? Or who you may even turn into the police, depending upon the severity of their transgressions?

There can be a lot of complicated feelings to work through when dealing with our ancestors, but there are ways to have a full and well-rounded spiritual life as a pagan, without immersing ourselves in damaging ancestral trauma or shame.

Those Who Came Before

Genealogy is a big trend in the 21st century. Sites which help you look up your family tree or even check your DNA are all the rage, as people look to find a connection to the past. For those pagans on a path that includes ancestor worship, it's never been easier to make that connection to those who came before. For a fee, companies will look up names and places to give greater detail into the lives of antecedents. People can find out what jobs their ancestors held, what political parties they were part of, and how they contributed towards their communities.

This is great news when it includes discovering that you have mixed heritage from a hundred interesting countries, or that your great-great-grandmother was the head of a charity or a proponent for women's rights. However, it becomes more of a disturbing experience when you discover things you wish had been left buried. Although hiding from the past is never a good idea, it can be completely understandable why it may be a shock for a pagan to find out that the ancestors they have been honouring were not, in fact, all that great.

This can lead to great internal turmoil, as the person with this new information has to decide whether they should continue to include that ancestor within their spiritual lives. Reasons beloved ancestors may be a little less beloved after some careful research:

Slavery
Murder
Rape
Abuse
Violence
Harmful greed (e.g. wealthy landowner who let others die in
    poverty)
Harmful politics
Homophobia
Racism
Other harmful prejudices

There could be many more reasons why you decide an ancestor isn't worthy of your respect or veneration. These will differ depending on your own moral code and set of ethics. It can be useful to look at the time that the person was alive, and what was expected from them within the society they lived in. However, this doesn't have to be a way to justify their behaviour. If you find out an ancestor did something you cannot condone, you should never be expected to just brush it under the carpet or laugh it off.

I read a piece on Patheos (an online collection of blogs focused on religion and spirituality) recently that said it was potentially unjust to cut ancestors out of your life completely. It suggested that in several hundred years, our actions may be considered appalling by our ancestors, so we should be careful of being too judgemental. Our descendants may find somethings that we do repulsive, even though we consider them perfectly acceptable in today's society. It also suggested that we have a duty to honour our ancestors, and that it was our 'obligation' to recover from ancestral wounds in order to be able to venerate them.

I have one response to that: No.

No, there is no obligation to venerate people who have caused irreparable damage to others.

No, there is no obligation to forgive or force yourself to be 'okay' with some terrible act, simply because it happened a long time ago, or because the person who committed the act is one of your ancestors.

No, it is not unjust to ostracise an ancestor from your spiritual life if they will only bring you distress or shame. Spirituality is about growth and connection, not about forcing yourself to accept things that are, to your soul, truly unacceptable.

If you look at someone in your past and feel nothing but disgust, then there is no shame, no shame at all, in purposefully excluding them from any ancestral worship. This isn't about forgetting them or ignoring the terrible things they did, but it could absolutely be about purposefully saying, "I refuse to honour you and your place in my lineage."

But what if your path demands ancestral veneration? What if it would make you feel more uncomfortable to pick and choose the ancestors you honour? This is where the turmoil occurs; the internal debate or conflict between religious duty and moral duty. In that situation, there are a few things you can do to include your entire line of ancestors, without placing praise or honour upon the person or people who genuinely do not deserve it.

Simple acknowledgement

If you feel the need to call to all of your ancestors, perhaps to show gratitude for your existence or to send love and respect back down your ancestral line, a simple acknowledgement of the ancestor's existence may be enough. You don't need to praise them. You don't need to make much of their achievements or lack of. You don't even need to focus on the things they did that appalled you or made you feel shame. Simply name them, acknowledge their existence, and move on to the next ancestor. Perhaps name them in relation to their descendants or direct ancestors, thus giving them a place in your family line without assigning any place of power to them.

I recognise (name), child of (name) and parent of (name), ancestor of mine.

This simple acknowledgement shows that you are fully aware of their place within your lineage, and its importance in the grand scheme of your existence. But by failing to acknowledge any more detail about them or their life, you are removing any power they may have over you.

41

Focus on something they did that you can honour

This one is a little trickier, but it can help you get past the awful things they did. By focusing on something the ancestor did that makes you happy or proud, you can honour that aspect of them that has now manifested itself in your own life.

For example, if there is an account of them being a great parent, despite terrible homophobic tendencies, you could say:

I am grateful to my ancestor (name) whose skill with parenting was passed down through the generations to me.

If it's a skill that has nothing at all to do with you, you could honour it anyway:

I honour my ancestor, (name), whose skill as a blacksmith benefited their whole community.

You don't need to ignore the bad things they did. In fact, you shouldn't, as historical whitewashing is very damaging and can cause us to be less aware of our own behaviour. But by focusing on the more positive aspects of their lives, you may be able to include them in your ancestral veneration without feeling undue distress.

Condemnation

You can accept an ancestor as part of your lineage without being happy with them at all. If you are confident that you want to honour your entire ancestral line, that you are aware of, then it may be worth fully accepting their acts and condemning them accordingly. Do your research, get all the facts together, then when you are ready to honour your ancestors you will be fully armed to let this one know exactly what you think of them:

Ancestor of mine, (name), I am ashamed that a member of my

42

family has acted so. I recognise your deeds and I condemn them, in the hope that they may never be repeated by a member of my family or one of my descendants.

This reminds you (and your ancestors) of who is alive right now and who has the power to make real change in the world, via their decisions and actions. Never fear that you will become your ancestors. No matter how shameful their actions, you have the power to be a completely different person.

You could combine these methods, or use these ideas to come up with your own way of dealing with ancestral shame. If you are part of a group or coven that works together on ancestral ritual, it may be worth mentioning that you have ancestors that you are not comfortable with. A supportive group will understand if you need to change a ritual's wording, or omit parts of it all together. Make sure your group knows how important this is to you. It's easy to say, "It's in the past," and try and force forgiveness upon something that, in your mind and heart, is unforgiveable.

Don't be pressured into feeling like the issue is less than it is. When you are torn between spiritual duty and the abhorrent action of an ancestor, it's a very difficult situation and not to be taken lightly. Find a way that works for you, but ultimately, if an ancestor has a history that is too painful to deal with, then don't allow anyone to tell you that you should be including them in your life.

Those Who are Here Right Now

Ancestors aren't all dead, of course. Honouring your ancestors means honouring those who are around you right now, perhaps unavoidably. I hope that for most of you reading this, that this is a good thing. That you have positive relationships with your living ancestors, and that even if you don't speak or can't see each other, that it brings you no pain to light a candle in their honour, or to raise a glass in toast to them.

Sadly, this is not always the case. Living ancestors includes parents, grandparents, great-grandparents, carers, foster carers – the list goes on. Anyone who has had a formative influence on you could be included here. This may even include mentors and spiritual leaders or guides. There's a gut reaction in some pagan paths to suggest that these people are always deserving of honour, regardless of their actions. Here are just a few reasons why I disagree with that, and why these ancestors may have lost the right to any kind of inclusion or veneration:

Physical abuse
Emotional abuse
Sexual abuse
Gaslighting
Bullying
Destruction of self-esteem
Refusal to accept (religion, sexuality, gender, politics etc.)
Violence to others (including but not limited to siblings, other
    parents/carers)
Criminal activity
Destructive beliefs (holocaust denial, trying to 'cure' autistic
    people etc.)

This is not an exhaustive list but I hope it serves to highlight the fact that just because someone is related to you, that does not give them special privileges. Just because someone fed and clothed you, it doesn't mean you have to honour them if they are, in fact, a horrible person. It's OK to be grateful for the things they did for you and then move past that. It's OK to accept that someone was a part of your life, but that they don't need to be anymore. It's OK to walk away from someone who is causing you to be ill, distressed, deeply unhappy – particularly if you've tried to resolve any issues and been made to feel like you are the one in the wrong.

Dealing with living ancestors who hold sway over you is traumatic enough without feeling pressured to include them in your spiritual practice. Someone who has made you feel like a victim is not someone who is going to enhance your religious path. Someone who has abused you is not going to be made welcome by a supportive deity. Someone who has never believed in you is not going to fit in well with a path that includes daily affirmations of your own self-worth.

There are constructive and helpful ways to take the focus away from people who make you uncomfortable or cause you distress, whether they are living or long dead.

Focus on an ancestor you love or admire who matches your morals or ethics.

If, as part of your spiritual or religious path, you have to meditate on the ancestors or perform a ritual to honour the ancestors, you don't have to blanket honour them all. In fact, when you have ancestors who don't deserve this, it can ruin your experience as your mind can be invaded by thoughts and memories that make you unhappy or anxious. Spirituality and religion are not always easy, but one would hope that walking your path should not be a traumatic experience. Reliving past trauma is a terrible result of religion and one that most pagans would be particularly wary of.

An alternative to this is to avoid the blanket ancestral worship, and instead, focus on a particular ancestor or set of ancestors that you are comfortable with. This could be a grandparent who always had your back. It could be the parent who looked out for you, or who tried their best to protect you. It could even be a more abstract definition of an ancestor, like a favourite teacher, or a school counsellor who really understood you and your struggle. Whoever it is, choose someone who has had a positive influence in your life, and who doesn't make you feel discomfort or shame. Focus on why you are proud to have them as an ancestor. If they are still alive, what do they do that makes you happy? How do they contribute towards your life, and the lives of others around them?

In my path, we often focus on the ancestors at Samhain, the Celtic start of winter. We talk about our ancestors, we leave photos of them out with offerings, and we make a 'dumb supper.' We set a table for the ancestors we wish to make welcome, and we lay out some of their favourite dishes. For those honouring ancestors further back in their lineage, these offerings might be less specific and more focused on their particular faith. Common Celtic offerings are mead, honey, and apples. The reason I love the dumb supper is that we only invite specific guests. It's not a free-for-all. We are saying, "You, my beloved ancestor(s), are special to me and it is you, specifically, that I wish to share my food and time with."

This has the dual purpose of bringing us closer to those we miss, but also protecting us from the spirits or energy of those who have caused us harm. Think about a family gathering. Would you invite a parent who had stolen from you and shown no remorse? Would you invite a carer who had constantly told you that you would amount to nothing? Would you invite the grandparent who had tried to stab your brother? One would hope not. So why would you invite people like this to a spiritual gathering?

It's important to remember that just because a person has died, they are not automatically absolved of all their sins. That might be the dogma in some more mainstream religions, but I cannot believe that we are just expected to forgive someone simply because they are no longer with us. I appreciate that forgiveness can be very healing, and that it can be seen as a way to heal ancestral wounds. However, even when forgiveness has been given, it does not imply any obligation to associate with a spirit or person that has performed terrible acts or deeds.

I want to end by saying that whatever your path, whatever

your spirituality or beliefs, you owe absolutely nothing to any ancestor that makes you feel uncomfortable or traumatised. Never, ever feel pressured to include anyone in your religious or spiritual life who didn't earn their place there.

There's a popular line of thought that we are all the results of the decisions our ancestors made. And, of course, that's true to a certain extent. Your ancestor's decisions may have led to your physical appearance on this world. But it's your decisions and actions that determine the person you are today. You are not beholden to your ancestors, and even if you do feel some debt of gratitude, it's OK to keep that totally separate from your opinion of them as people, as individuals, and as an influence in your life.

If you need to cut someone out of your life for your own mental health or physical safety, a supportive pagan path will never make you feel guilty for doing so. If you have to disregard a whole section of your ancestry in order to make Samhain or other festivals a less traumatic event, do it. Focus on what matters to you; what you consider to be right and true. You may be the culmination of your ancestors, the very front of your ancestral line, but your life is yours and yours alone. You have the chance to break away from ancient enmities, to condemn historical actions, and to change the course of your living history. Focus on making your own life one that your descendants will be proud to honour.

And if it anyone tells you they you *should* be honouring ancestors you cut ties with long ago, smile and simply walk away.

Mabh Savage lives in Yorkshire, England, and explores her heritage as a way to get closer to the world around her, and understand her ancestors more. She is the author of *A Modern Celt* and *Celtic Witchcraft*.

Ancestral Healing

Elen Sentier

Ancestral Healing – ways of reinvigorating and rebuilding, enabling the land, her creatures and people to be restored to health that have been passed down, inherited, through the people, the folk, the family. These are available in Britain as they are in every land all around the world; we have our old, shamanic ways, they're just very well hidden and often in plain sight. After all, we have had to hide for over 2000 years now so we're pretty good at it!

Ancestral, for me, is about family but this goes far, far wider that just the blood-bonds of my current lifetime; and healing takes me into ideas of recovering, restoring, rebuilding and reinvigorating the old wisdom of my people. My people, my folk, my tylwyth to use one of our old words for people, is the people who brought me up and educated me, taught me so much about how to *live-with* the world. In order to survive and mitigate the times we all live in right now, climate change and all that means for every single being on Planet Earth, means we must learn again how our ancestors did this so much better than most of us do now.

Way back in the 1950s, I was brought up by my family and the elders (older pagan folk) of the villages we lived in on Dartmoor and on the edge of Exmoor, in Britain. Looking back now, it's incredible to me just how much change has happened in the intervening years, and how very different the world is now. We really need the old ancestral ways to help us find our way through climate change, and help the Earth to become whole again.

So, what is ancestral healing for me? It's about getting back together with our old ways of living-with and working-with, and that's hard because attitudes have changed so much over the past 250 years and especially during my lifetime. For thousands of years there has always been an element of greed in human nature but this seems to have really speeded up since the Industrial Revolution; that's just 250 years ago as it's said to have begun around 1760.

It's deeply connected with the Age of Enlightenment, and that happened all around the same time. Many consider Descartes' 1637 statement *I think, therefore I am* to have sparked the Age of Enlightenment, while French historians traditionally date the Enlightenment from 1715, the beginning of Louis XV reign, up to 1789 and the French Revolution. Whatever the dates, the thinking The Enlightenment projected changed human attitudes enormously; and that thinking has pervaded all of life and living to such an extent it's become de rigueur and normal for most people. We became completely materialistic; profit and making money are what drives people's lives and ambitions, even those who protest it doesn't will find – if they look closely – that their mores and morals are infested with these ideas. Money has become the main thing in the minds of all civilised westernised people. Nowadays, even disasters like the Boxing Day tsunami are measured first of all in dollars, not lives, or damage to the environment but how much monetary value they have chopped off somebody's scale! We treat our Planet as a commodity to be extorted, squeezed until there is no life left in her, used and made into an acceptable safe place for our terrified society. For me, that's terrible.

And that's all come about since we became materialistic. True, it began when a strange middle eastern religion began to tell people that humans were god's highest creation; and that likely grew out of the ownership we all learned once we began farming, that led to mine/yours, I want yours, I'll kill you to get it. Ouch! But boy, did we take that up several orders of magnitude with the Industrial Revolution!

Our old ways aren't like that. We don't impose on the natural world, we don't try to rule and command Mother Earth, nor Father Sky, nor the universe, nor anything. We ask and listen and learn from them ... for they are our Elders.

I've been deeply moved by the kids this year of 2019. Since Greta Thunberg got noticed and has been able to offer her thoughts on TV and the internet all over the world, the kids have got a voice. Even out here in the wilds of the Welsh Marches the kids went marching past the hairdresser's when I was there the other week, and me and my hairdresser went out to cheer them on. Well done kids, I just so hope people really do take notice of you, that the establishment doesn't succeed in burying you in the processes of normality, the old *the adults know best* syndrome. As I expect you've guessed, I grew up in the 1960s, another time of rebellion, and we did manage to do some good back then, attitudes to war for instance with the Viet Nam protests, Women's Lib too, and Human Rights. But kids today have even more reason to try to change attitudes all over the world; we are not going to escape climate change, however much we may try to bury our heads in the sand. It's already happening all around us. The kids have noticed, now the adults have to learn to notice too. The old platitudes from politicians and business men will not suffice any more – we have to change our whole belief system and our attitudes.

What has this to do with ancestral healing? For me, everything. The old shamanic ways of every country, every land, in the world come from the times when we all *lived-with* our Earth, instead of living on her and off her as we do now. Civilised people all over the world have this disconnect from nature, from the natural world, they're afraid of wasps and spiders, they want netting put up at supermarkets so they don't get bird-poo on them, they're happy with hedges being netted so birds have nowhere to live; they cannot bear to share their lives with any of the larger animals, make up daft stories about foxes carrying off babies from their cots. People have no concept of living with nature, except in a nicely curated town park or zoo, or maybe watching wildlife programmes on TV. But live there? What me? Shock horror run.

Our old ways here in Britain all encourage us to reconnect with the natural world. We need this, so very much. We need to heal the ancestral break, the cut-off, that has come about since we have become more and more materialistic, and our old ways from all around the world can help us to reconnect. As a species, we humans will not survive unless we do so.

Here in Britain, our old ways are all about this connection. We know ourselves to be the youngest species on Planet Earth; we know everything else is older than us, so we know everything else is our Elder from whom we can learn. This is what we all need to relearn; and it's there, available for us in whatever land we now live in; the old ways are always there … but you must search for them with your heart, not your head!

But do most people? Mostly not. People think animals and birds are less intelligent than us … but science is now showing us just how wrong this attitude is. Have you seen the internet videos of crows solving problems many kids and adults would fail at? Similarly, have you seen the videos of elephants and ravens mourning, of the baby bats crying as their mother's fall out of the Australian trees in the horrific drought of 2018 – and that drought was just one tiny result of climate change. No, we need to see all these things that break our hearts – only through a broken heart can real change come, when we know-in-our-bones that things have gone completely wrong. Then we can follow our hearts to find the ways to enable the Earth, the land, her creatures and people, to be restored to health

To do this we must return to our old ways; heal the ancestral break that we made when we left the path of Life to follow the path of greed and materialism. We must learn again to know everything else in creation is of equal importance to ourselves, deserving just the same attention, rights and privileges we grant ourselves. Since World War II we have begun to climb out of racism and we've mostly dropped the idiotic eugenics ideas that inspired Hitler. We (most of us) no longer think of some races as *unmenschlich* – the word the Nazis used for what they called sub-human people, like Jews, Russians, gay people, gipsies, blacks. Now, we must drop *speciesism*. We must stop thinking that anything not human, any other species than humanity, is less than ourselves.

In the old ways, equality of all things prevails all over the Earth. So, what can we all do? Learn, learn, learn about everything non-human – every plant, animal, bird, fish; every insect, bug, microbe, virus; every single atom. We all need to come to understand just how inextricably intertwined we are all are. We cannot continue to only allow homogenised, castrated, nature as the only thing we can live with; we must learn to know-in-our-bones that we are all part of the same creation.

In our old ways here in Britain we do know it; we have a funny old song that says it all perfectly, On Ilkley Moor Bhat'at. It tells the story of a young lassie who goes a'courting on a wild wet night on the moor of Ilkley in Yorkshire; of how she catches her death of cold, dies and gets buried, how the worms eat up her body, how the ducks eat the worms, and how we (her family) eat the ducks. So it ends …

Then we shall all 'ave etten thee
On Ilkla Moor baht 'at
Then we shall all 'ave etten thee
That's wheer we get us oahn back
On Ilkla Moor baht 'at
That's wheer we get us own back

Yup … that says it all, it really does. Every atom that makes up the bodies we wear in our current lifetimes has been an atom of something else. That cabbage you had for dinner last night will go through you, get composted (hopefully) and go back around again, become part of a butterfly maybe, or a cow. Then when you die, your current body will go back to being atoms again to become part of a cabbage perhaps, or a butterfly or a cow. Think about that. Your spirit will go on to another life, in another physical body, perhaps made of some of those same atoms that make up you now. It will gain more experience for you to upload into the universal cloud that is all experience ... not just human experience but the experience of everything. That includes stars and planets as well as trees and cows and people; like Joni Mitchell sang, *We are stardust, we are golden* ... and we really do need to remember that.

What will knowing all that do for us? Change our attitudes; and with attitude change comes complete economic and political change – that's the scary bit! My Aged Parent (Dad, now deceased) used to grin wryly and quote an old World War I joke; this older bloke in a shell hole on the Somme is talking to a younger bloke who's moaning about how bad everything was; the old bloke says to the young one, "If you knows of a better hole, you go to it". People are like that, they moan about how bad things are but if it comes down to really changing, changing their life completely, they knuckle down and stick with the status quo rather than change, and often with a phrase like, "it can't get any worse". Oh yes it can, and it is.

We have to change. We have to learn to care about everything else. We have to stop making money both a god to be worshipped and a commodity to be amassed. It was never intended as either; it was originally a means of exchange and it needs to go back to being that again. We don't even really want money, we want to be happy, content, but we've been conned and educated into believing we need to buy-buy-buy, in order to make this true. Of course, that doesn't work. We amass huge piles of things yet are even more miserable as we struggle on with our burden of work-

work-work so we can buy-buy-buy. What was it the Beatles sang? Can't buy me love. No more you can.

The old ways show you this. You learn what our ancestors (even as near ago as in the 1950s and 60s) knew, like the joy of a sunrise, a robin singing his evensong, a mumuration of starlings across the sunset, a fox watching you from behind a tree, a curious wolf sniffing into your tent, a panther crossing your path when you're out for a walk. Yes, all these things you can watch on the internet, they've really happened to real people. Maybe you've had a chaffinch take crumbs from your hand, remember how that felt? Bet you held your breath. Our old ways include all these things as part of learning how to be, how to BE with the Earth. Would you like that?

Most people would. If they could find a way to have a roof over their heads and food in their bellies, and for their families, would be content. They don't need a new iPhone, a new car, a new washing machine. But to get there we must stop wanting money; and we won't do that without we help everyone else to stop wanting it too.

The kids have this idea, it's what they want; they want people to care about everything. And, despite what most adults think, they do understand what this means. They also know it means horrible things like continuous competition at school would be things of the past too. Gone would be all that examination, competition, catch-up stress that comes from parents continuously telling them must do better or they won't survive. They know only that's only true when you buy into all the rest of the capitalist crap most folk live by.

We have to heal ourselves. We have to relearn the attitudes of our ancestors; learn how to make it all work without losing grip on the reality of the old ways, the way of loving and knowing the connectedness of everything. We must stop making ourselves separate.

The beginning of doing that is to stop saying helplessly, "but what can we do?" We change ourselves. Like Greta Thunberg, we go and sit outside the Swedish parliament, all on our own if necessary, then next day others join in, and others and others. So, let's change, let's relearn our old ways, our old thinking and attitudes. Let's begin our Ancestral Healing.

Elen Sentier is the author of a number of bestselling books on British native shamanism including *Elen of the Ways*, *The Celtic Chakras* and *Trees of the Goddess*.

Stuck in the Rage Stage?

Dorothy Abrams

I was taking to a college student the other day who insisted she had never been discriminated against nor victimized by sexual violence. That would be a delightful life were it true. I knew her boyfriend had hit her more than once. She had been mauled on campus by two men but escaped further assault through the intervention of a third man. She had been denied time off at work when her male counterpart received generous time off to hang out with his girlfriend. She had been berated by the same boss for being slow, stupid and female. Previously she had a job that included sexual advances. She walked out. Yet she insisted she had not been targeted because she's a woman. She is in denial. Many of us start out that way.

The fact is nearly every woman has had some sort of unwanted sexual advance. Most of us have been on the receiving end of anger, blaming and hurtful words designed to keep us in our place and to undercut our confidence. Many of us have experienced harm at the hands of our family: spankings, a slap across the face, physical pain born of adult resentment. For some it is incest. And what do we do with all that? We stuff it inside. We take it to heart. We learn the erroneous lesson that this is all somehow our fault. What we are trained not to do is get angry at the perpetrators.

Ironically that is exactly what we need. Anger. The first step in healing violence against women is to name the violence for what it is. The second step is to get angry about it.

I am a women's advocate, retired. I have been part of a team that established a domestic violence shelter and another team that established a rape crisis center. I worked as an investigator of civil rights complaints including those based on sexual harassment and which were initiated within the legal system. I am also a witch. I've spent a life time working to create equal, safe opportunities for women in their spiritual, personal and professional lives. The pain and suffering left behind by the denial of these rights is part of my blood and bones. I am angry. I am angry for all the bullshit heaped on these women and myself. I could not remain stuck in the rage stage if I were to live. I have had to turn my life into a healing journey or die trying. The fact is, to heal from the violence, we need to name it, name our anger and use both to create something new. That journey is aided by the power of the witch.

My healing is a direct-approach healing. I know wise people have offered paths of forgiveness, confrontation, group therapy, meditation or medication. Those seem the long way around Robin Hood's Barn. What I did with myself and many others takes the named outrageous behavior, dips it deep into a woman's rage and then makes something of it. Something like a witch's circle, a crisis intervention program, a political campaign, a book, articles, art or music. Something wild. Something dynamic. Something that moves us out of the rage stage. When the anger settles down from white hot rage to a sense of satisfaction in a job well done, we know we made the crossing from wounded crazy woman to a powerful conduit of Goddess energy.

So how is that done? We tell our stories. We make certain we are heard and understood. We name our anger and identify its sources. Then we get together with other women and build something to respond to those sources. Meanwhile we seek information on how to succeed with this project. Women have walked this path before. How did they do it? We create rituals to fit our needs. We gather energy from our group and send it out with a social conscience like a cone of power. We assess our healing process against our emotions and physical health. We ask for help when we are stuck or discouraged. We know we take two steps forward and on step back but we never give up.

We change the community around us and we save ourselves.

As I write this essay, *The Washington Post* printed an article about a woman being grabbed when she was out running. She was angry. She pressed charges. She expected the perpetrator to be punished. He was given two weeks of jail time served on weekends so it didn't interfere with his work. Please. That is no deterrent. The sentence gives no healing. Her comment after pursuing justice whole heartedly was that she had not been running for two years ever since he jumped her. Sometimes our advocacy is not rewarded.

At that point she ramped up her campaign and notified the restaurants this man worked in that he was a predator. Women stepped up and spoke against him too. The restaurant business is rife with sexual abuse of employees. He lost his job, but of course he found another. That was a partial healing. Then she told her story to the newspapers. She has been heard.

Finding a forum to speak our truth without mansplaining, judgment and blaming the victim can be a challenge. One of the first things we can create in our healing is a forum where we are heard. This can be done in ritual space with a cast circle or not.

Ritual: I encourage women to find two trusted friends who also have stories to tell and use a process I learned from noted feminist Sonia Johnson: Hearing into Being. Women select groups of three to sit in and tell their stories. Each one speaks for twenty minutes uninterrupted. One keeps time. The other keeps eye contact and gives positive body language. Nodding, breathing together, offering tissues, or a hand over the heart encourages the woman to keep talking. Twenty minutes sounds like a long time. It isn't. Listeners do not interrupt, ask questions, offer their own experience, comfort or help. This is the speaker's story. She alone owns it.

At the end of twenty minutes everyone changes roles. The speaker becomes the time keeper. The time keeper becomes the listener. The listener becomes the speaker. Without discussion, but maybe with silent hugs among the three women, they enter into the next twenty minutes and then the next. The circle comes together afterward to talk about their experience in being heard, not about what people said. Our words are confidential. participants talk about how they felt as time keeper, listener and speaker. They describe how it felt to be heard and believed.

Story telling opens the soul to its own stored rage. Knowing people have heard you and understood is a first step, but how can that be shaped into something healing? That depends on the woman.

A survivor of violence tells her story repeatedly until she believes and recognizes it for what it is: part of a pattern of bias directed against women across recorded time and place. She learns about women married off against their will (my grandmother), raped by their boyfriends (me) or husbands, abused by men within the family (perhaps you), accosted by men in the street (most of us) and then paid unequally in employment, denied control over their own reproductive health, questioned and cross questioned then disbelieved when we disclose our experiences. People finally blame survivors for not fighting hard enough, not bargaining hard enough, not being careful, or failing to dress right.

Make no mistake about it. All of these experiences are a violent severing of our confident girl self from our potent woman witch self in order to prevent us from being great. All of this history exists on our inner continuum of anger. To access the power of that inner scale, I ask women to write anger words down on paper. In sacred space, draw a horizontal line and arrange those anger words on the line from least to most. If the words will not come, use meditation and automatic writing to access the hidden feelings connected to your history. What words would you use? The building of a vocabulary of rage is different for each of us.

Most women begin with *uncomfortable* or *upset*. I am upset when_____. Fill in the blank with an experience you have had.

When I have to walk by a construction site and ignore wolf whistles or crude comments like "Baby, I got what you want. Come over here."

The next level might be *mad*. I am so mad when____. What about everyday living as a woman irritates you? Are you mad when you work all day and then come home to fix dinner while the family watches TV? Or when you offer a suggestion to a group only to have it ignored until a man floats it back as his own idea? Or when you direct an employee who ignores you until they are told the same thing by a man? Yeah, those things make me mad.

Then we might graduate to angry. What really gets under your skin? What pushes your buttons so you count to 10 before speaking? What would happen if you didn't count to 10? Is it when some politico makes a sexist remark laughing about grabbing women by their private parts or kissing them by surprise just because he can? Is it reading about other women's experiences and recognizing them as your own? Is it hearing people criticize survivors of abuse for not coming forward sooner? Or blaming the victim as if she had it coming, and knowing you did not? What do you do with that anger? How do you speak out? What happens when you do?

Further along the anger continuum is *outrage*. What makes you ready to pound the table with your shoe, but you don't because you would undercut whatever credibility you had? Is it seeing a woman vilified for testifying against an appointed official who violated her in the past? Is it an assault on your sister or your daughter? What pushes you past *outrage* into *fury*? Is it an assault on you yourself? Or does that deflate the ballooning fury because it's okay, I can handle it.

Any of us who defuses our own violation as okay and expects to handle matters internally gets stuck in the rage stage. We step up to the edge of the abyss and back away. What if they blame me? What if they don't hear me? What if they don't believe me?

What if I sink into my rage and can't return? What if I go insane? Recognize those questions as fears but keep on going.

Healing our history and rage, changing our stories to include restoration of me and you lead us into our creativity. I suggest using creative space to rewrite our outcomes. Even if, like the woman in the Post's story, we pursue legal action and fail our creativity can re-write and correct that disempowerment.

Ritual: In a sacred circle with others on this healing journey, ground and center. Descend into the dark past and remember. Then call out loud phrases that are powerful responses to the perpetrator. I saw his face. I looked him in the eye. I kicked him in the balls. I called the cops. I told my mother. I told my father. I said NO! Imagine those responses worked. Sit with that vision until it feels possible. Maybe you could not do any of those things. Maybe you did and it didn't work. But right now, in sacred space, imagine it did. Call in the Goddess who will help you make that work. Feel her power run in your veins. Be convinced that the assault was not your fault. Society's failure to act is not your fault.

When it's time someone asks "What is the next step?" Again, still half in trance, call out answers. I testified in court. I made flyers to warn other women. I took a friend and confronted him face to face. I wrote a story for the newspaper. I gathered women together to form a crisis center. I organized a Take Back the Night March. I made protective amulets for myself, the women in the circle and my family. I wrote a book. The possibilities are endless for creative confrontation of the rape culture. A group that shares collective ideas can select one and make it happen together. Come back to ordinary consciousness and talk about group choices.

If you begin this process alone you will need allies. Testifying in court? You need supporters in the courtroom. Passing around flyers? You need helpers to cover the neighborhood. Confronting a perpetrator? You need someone to assess the safety and who will help provide security. Some of these people can and will do violence. Women die at the hands of their perps. Our rage must not lead us into more violence. We need numbers of allies to establish crisis centers or a rally against fear. Joining other women and working a collective project to make the world safer is a healing step in trust. Women aren't encouraged to feel rage. Neither are they encouraged to trust other women.

Once the living women have selected an action, we engage our ancestral mothers. I mentioned my grandmother who was forced into a marriage. I know her story because she told me. On the other side of the family the women had asthma and respiratory ailments. I do too. Physically healing that chain of airlessness has been tough. I learned their stories in meditation, travelling through time to find them and hear their stories. One saw her husband fall in love with her nurse. Another left the old country and knew her mother died alone, gasping for air. Her husband had left her cold and hungry. Another died in childbirth after working too hard without enough food to sustain her life or the baby's. Her daughter brought up the child. One was attacked by her father-in-law. Another was hit by her husband. All of this collective grief cut off their breath. Their healing rested on me to find a way to weather the coughing and wheezing.

Why me? Perhaps because medical science has powerful medicines that open airways now. Or because I studied the Craft and learned how to astral travel to them for the stories. Maybe my study of acupressure helped them as it helped me. One thing especially stands out. I set a ritual circle for myself and all the grandmothers back seven generations. We held hands. We sent our energy spiraling around and up into the Cosmos to explode, It showered down healing and a release of old grudges to set each of us free in our own centuries. Our lungs were infused with white light. Our hearts were strengthened. Our minds stilled. We glowed with the Great Radiant Goddess Mother. We grew healthier.

I still do a white light meditation in the morning. It's a full body experience so light from the moon, stars and sun settles into every cell of my body. It clears out mucus and inflammation. I breathe deeply and thankfully. I see the line of grandmothers extending back in time doing the same. I take bronchodilators for them as well as me. We also tell our stories. One of my ancestors came up off the bed and hit him back. He had a broken tooth and never hit her again. One kicked her lecherous father-in-law out of the house and gave her husband the choice: him or me. One died and let the nurse have him. The Summerland was more beautiful than the pain betrayal gave her. Another watched over her daughters as a guardian from the spirit world. Me? I made agencies happen that would help other women find their way through the pain. I write. I teach.

One thing is clear. None of us are still stuck in the rage stage. We have moved our anger into something else. We have changed the world. Yet women still experience discrimination and violence. Like my student-friend, they are struck by their boyfriends, mauled on campus, harassed at work, undercut by verbal abuse, and in some cases raped. It is true, even in the presence of magic. If we are to heal the wounds in our blood and bones, we need more ritual, more stories, more women standing in their power and telling the truth. We need to find the Rage Stage and then move through it.

Dorothy Abrams is the co-founder of the Web PATH Center, a pagan church and teaching center in Lyons, New York USA, and the author of *Identity and the Quartered Circle*.

Looking them in the Eyes: Animals, Ancestry and Animism

Andrew Anderson

During the excavations at Shakespeare's New Place in Stratford-upon-Avon, the team found many animal bones. Not all of them are on display to the public, but there is one piece of cattle bone which has become very special to me. It is part of a leg bone from a cow which was reared on the site, slaughtered and butchered on site and eaten by those who lived there. The bone itself tells that story clearly as, just visible on its mottled white surface, is the thin slice of a cleaver where the animal's flesh was stripped away when it was butchered.

One of the reasons that particular bone has become so special to me is because her whole story can be seen in that six-inch remnant of her body. However, I also find it fascinating because it speaks of a very different way of treating animals. That she lived her entire life on the site at New Place, probably being born and raised from the Shakespeare stock, ties her specifically to that piece of land. Her life would have been ended only when she was needed to feed the family. In the past, animal's lives had value because they were there to sustain the community through tough times. To kill one of your stock unnecessarily could be perilous and mean the difference between eating and starvation further through the winter. Going even further back, this is one of the reasons why animal sacrifices were so meaningful; slaughtering a lamb was the equivalent of slaughtering a small child, the community relied on them that much. The word 'animal' itself derives from the Latin 'anima', which simply means 'soul', a term which includes humans and animals equally. It is very much in that shared sense of 'soul' that I use the term animal in this essay. That sense of value is crucial to the cow who lived at New Place. It's not so much that Shakespeare ate the cow's meat I find interesting, but that he probably looked her in the eye when she was grazing on his land.

That sense of respect, that closeness to the animal members of our community, has certainly changed. The industrialisation of farming turned our farmed animals into produce, a component part in an international feeding machine whose lives are ended at the demand of a consumer who has never looked into their eyes. For many people, there is a disconnect between the animal they see in the field and the meat they have on their plate or in their sandwich. They are unable, or unwilling, for whatever reason, to fully grasp that the lambs they see frolicking in the fields in early spring are running around on the legs that adorn their Sunday lunch table shortly after, that those young lives will be ended prematurely so that they can overeat and fall asleep in front of the television. We've all encountered people who 'comedically' shout "Mint sauce" at a field full of lambs but who, if push came to shove, couldn't actually kill the animal themselves. We are a society who never look our cattle, or, to put it crudely, our lunch, in the eye.

It is that sense of personal disconnection which led to me becoming vegetarian and, latterly, vegan. During Christmas adverts for three-bird roasts I began to question whether it was right that three animals had to die so that someone could eat one meal. Living close to the Cotswolds, I became acutely aware of the lorryloads of animals on the roads being transported to the slaughterhouses. Interestingly, during the period I began toying with the idea of vegetarianism, I found myself following more and more of these lorries along the roads, almost as if my conscience was pricking me to take note of the industrialised process in which I was complicit. The turning point for me came when I ended up in a traffic jam on the motorway, sandwiched in between a lorryload of cows heading to slaughter on my left and a butcher's refrigerated van on my right. I guess, as I hadn't embraced the connection for myself, synchronicity decided to spell it out clearly for me! As the deep, hazel eyes peered from the slots in the lorry to my left, I was given no choice but to look back at them and I didn't like the fear I saw there.

A couple of years ago I became vegan. I am, what I believed is called, an ethical vegan, someone who doesn't believe animals should be exploited for the benefit of humans. However, I would also class myself as a pragmatic vegan. This means that I recognise that I am lucky enough to live in a time when being vegan is incredibly easy and so it is a choice I have been able to make. It also means that I am aware that the day may come when, if I can ensure that they are treated ethically, I may begin to eat some animal products again. For example, I have often thought I would like to keep chickens and would eat the eggs they laid (although my doctor may not be so happy as veganism means I have a wonderfully low cholesterol level for a middle-aged man!). It is the industrialisation of farming, the lack of respect and sense of waste which I object to. This sense of pragmatism means I make it a point not to lecture people who currently eat animal products because, at the end of the day, it is a personal choice. We all have access to the same information; we can all find out what the processes and implications of industrial farming are; whether we chose to or not is a matter of individual conscience.

Additionally, there is a sense of guilt which stops me from hectoring others about their consumption of animal products. For most of my life, I was complicit in the system I now oppose. I used to meat. Even during the period when I started to become aware of the lorryloads of animals, I'd push the image from my head before ordering a medium rare steak on a night out. As veganism has grown and become fodder for media outlets, there has been an increase in pundits labelling their vegan guests as hypocrites for previously eating meat or for killing millions of insects through their plant-based diet. While this may grab headlines, the accusation of hypocrisy for a vegan is nothing compared to the deep sense of personal culpability and shame we feel from having participated in the system ourselves. I may not have indulged in a three-bird roast, but at least two animals died so I could snack on a chicken and bacon sandwich. The name calling and derision from other people is nothing compared to turning your gaze inward and the dark night of the soul this kind of reflection can trigger.

While some people may find guilt to be useful, for me it can be a heavy and paralysing emotion. I wanted to work more positively with my sense of personal responsibility towards the animals who had suffered and died for me in the past. The answer came from an idea explored by Stephen D Farmer in his book "Earth Magic". In a discussion on the influence of ancestors, Farmer states that human DNA does not disappear when we die but, upon burial, works its way into the landscape and ecosystem of our burial place. Reflecting on these ideas, I began to wonder if the human body works in the same way as the Earth and that, instead of simply expelling their DNA, the essence of the animals we have eaten works its way into our muscles, bones and sinews. Following this idea led me to a magical conclusion; if an animal has historically contributed to the make-up of my body, it is the equivalent of a human ancestor.

This realisation means that we can work far more positively with our consumed animal ancestors. It also changed my relationship with the New Place cattle bone. If Shakespeare did indeed eat that cow then, not only was she treated with more respect, as discussed above, but she also made her own contribution to the plays and poems of the world's greatest writer. Holding her remains is the equivalent of finding a piece of his mother or father, John Shakespeare and Mary Arden, or any of his ancestors, in the grounds of his home.

For me, this sense of animals as ancestors means that I have a far more positive way of honouring them and has opened up a number of possibilities for active and ongoing spiritual work in this area.

For some, honouring animals means activism. They expose the practices of the meat industry, in graphic detail, to shock people out of their complacency. The film *Earthlings*, made in 2005, is a well-known example of this, chronicling the exploitation of animals in a range of industries, not simply for food. Lately, so called 'radical vegans' have been accused of using shock tactics in their attempts to convert meat eaters, such as playing sounds from inside slaughter houses to unsuspecting passers-by. I have an immense respect for people who are able to carry out such work, but it is not something I could do. Seeing images of animals suffering simply overwhelms me with emotion and makes me incapable of any action at all. I have seen one piece of footage of a cow at the front of the queue, realising she is next for slaughter, and the look of terror in her eyes haunts me to this day. If you can undertake such work then I salute you, but for me, it strands me in the middle of that dark night of the soul I mentioned earlier.

Of course, to honour animals and their role as our ancestors does not mean that you have to be vegan or even vegetarian. In fact, eating meat makes the need to honour the animal it came from even more potent. I have always found the sense of "Saying Grace" intriguing, pausing before eating to thank, in the traditional Christian sense, God for providing the food. For me this becomes even more powerful when you honour the specific animal or animals for what their flesh will give you. Outside of prayer, there are more practical steps you can take to end the suffering of animals in the meat industry. Choosing meat from an ethical source does give animals a better quality of life than choosing mass reared and slaughtered meat. Of course, this type of meat comes with a higher price tag, which means that some people may find it difficult to purchase, and does need investigating further. Terms such as 'free-range' and 'ethically reared' are somewhat vague where the practice does not always live up to the image they conjure. Spending time finding out where your meat comes from, the conditions the animal has been kept in and the process of slaughter is a good first step towards honouring the soul who died so you can eat.

Some of the key practices for honouring human ancestors can work equally well when applied to our animal ancestors. In many cultures and traditions, honouring one's own body is a way of honouring your ancestors. For example, I had a very interesting conversation with a Japanese friend who seemed to find my piercings and tattoos problematic. He told me how, in Japanese culture, the body of an individual is a gift from their ancestors which needs to be taken care of. Therefore, he viewed actions such as tattooing and piercing as harmful to the body and, therefore, an insult to the ancestors. By focusing on our bodies as a place to honour our animal ancestors, we have a chance to work more positively with the legacy they have given us. While I don't eat animal products any more, elements of the souls I ate in my younger days remain within my body. They literally helped to make me into the person I am today. By staying healthy and eating well, I honour the gift they gave me and can use my body to actively campaign on their behalf. For example, the meat and produce my animal ancestors gave me has led to me writing this article. The belief that our animal ancestors are part of us, are within us, also brings them closer, dissolving the animal / human divide and harkening back to the original 'anima', the souls whose legacies live on through us.

One of the ways I honour my animal ancestors harkens back to the cattle bone from New Place. I was so taken with the fragment and the story it told that I decided to obtain a bone fragment to use as a focus for my spiritual work. Many of my friends use bones in their magical work, although they tend to use larger pieces, such as skulls. I wanted something non-descript, something which would be thrown away or given to a dog to chew on. I wanted to rescue something which would have been forgotten. I deliberately got the bone from a supermarket rather than a butcher, because I wanted it to come from an animal which had been part of the commercial food industry, a soul who no one had looked in the eye. This was a difficult decision as it meant, to some degree, I was perpetuating and condoning the meat industry. However, my intention remained to find something which would otherwise have been discarded as a way of remembering the generations of animals whose lives have been taken without gratitude or acknowledgement. This bone provides a focal point, a reminder of the animals I ate when I was younger, whose distant grandchildren now stand in the fields.

Of course, the most potent way of working with animals in the food industry is to get out into the fields and look them in the eye. Remember, it is important to do this safely and legally, ensuring you aren't trespassing on private land. There are a range of books and courses on animal communication, but just being with the animals is often enough. It fosters a sense of communion, further breaking down the human / animal divide and helps you to see the soul rather than the 'produce' they will become. In such situations it is always best to let the animals come to you, rather than forcing yourself upon them, and both you and the animals may find it more comfortable keeping the fence in between you for the first few meetings. If you are lucky enough to have fields near you which you can visit regularly, get to know the individuals in the group and sense their personalities. The problem with this kind of work is that there will come a day when the individuals are no longer there. They will have been taken on their final journey to the slaughterhouse. Some people have taken their work out of the fields and stand vigil at abattoirs, bearing witness to the suffering of animals at the end of their lives. You may ultimately feel that communicating and empathising with animals may be of little use as they will still end up finishing their lives on the conveyor belt of our meat industry, but that sense of being witness, of looking them in the eye, seeing them as another soul, is an incredibly important for both them and us. Every act of compassion, makes our world a better place, every connection forged breaks down a barrier and fosters change.

Within the central idea of this argument, that the animals we have eaten form part of our ancestry, lies a bigger truth. If it is the case that animals can be our ancestors, then surely the plants we eat are our ancestors too. And what about the water we drink? Here we reach the beautiful heart of animism, the multiplicity of souls and the interconnectedness of all.

Shakespeare himself, although constrained by the religious laws of his day, seemingly articulates animistic ideas in several of his plays, notably in *As You Like It* where Duke Senior describes the *"tongues in trees, books in the running brooks, / Sermons in stones, and good in everything."* Similarly, Caliban in *The Tempest* tells visitors, "Be not afeard. The isle is full of noises, / Sounds, and sweet airs, that give delight, and hurt not. / Sometimes a thousand twangling instruments / Will hum about mine ears, and sometime voices". Both of these plays were written after Shakespeare purchased New Place, and I like to think of him ruminating on concepts of animism as he made his way through his Warwickshire garden, before stopping to stare into the deep hazel eyes of one of his cows.

Andrew Anderson is a member of the Order of Bards, Ovates and Druids, a freelance English and Creative Writing teacher, and author of *The Ritual of Writing*.

Recovering the Bones, Healing the Past

Angela Paine

In every culture people need to witness and celebrate the various stages of life: birth, marriage and death. Death is possibly the most important stage to celebrate, be it through burning the body ceremonially and throwing the ashes into the Ganges, or some other holy river, as they do in India, or taking the body to church for a funeral with due pomp and ceremony and seeing the body, or coffin, laid to rest in a grave or tomb. All the friends and relatives of the dead accompany them to their last resting place and say goodbye. When a person disappears, there is no body to lay to rest, no one to mourn. The story of their life is left unfinished, incomplete and their relatives left wondering whether they will ever return, alive or dead.

Those who have not been properly mourned, whose bodies have not been buried or burned, linger in the collective unconscious of their descendants. People who have been bereaved but never seen the bodies or even the graves of their loved ones, search for them endlessly. This was the story of my grandfather, who lost his mother at sea and spent the rest of his life sailing out into the sea around the area where she drowned, off the coast of Alderney one of the Channel Islands.

He was a boy of thirteen, when the ship he was in, the Stella, hit the Casquets, dangerous rocks in the English Channel, on the way to the island of Guernsey. The Stella was one of two ferries that travelled from Southampton to Guernsey every day, in the late nineteenth century. The boats used to race because the first to arrive could enter the harbour, a space too small for two boats, thus unloading passengers and merchandise and heading back to Southampton, while the other boat waited outside the harbour. On this fateful day thick fog blanketed the sea and dripped from the railings. The captain was sure that he would hear the foghorn, warning him of the whereabout of the Casquets, and so steamed ahead. But the fog blanketed the sound of the foghorn as well as the sight of the rocks, so he hit the rocks and holed the ship, which very quickly sank.

My great grandmother, realising that she and her sons were too late to get into a life boat, tied a football to my grandfather's lapel. The boat upended and slid into the sea, sucking all who remained on deck down into the depths. My grandfather was pulled back up to the surface by his football and, seeing an upturned lifeboat, swam to it and clung there for dear life, as he searched the sea for his mother and brother. All around him bodies floated face downwards, in their cork lifebelts, while others clung to the life boat with him, like so many limpets on a wet rock.

Eventually a huge wave overturned the lifeboat and he was able to climb in with the few remaining survivors. He stayed, wet, cold and hungry, sitting in the lifeboat, half full of water, for twenty-three hours, as they drifted in the dark, stormy seas. He and his fellow survivors attempted to bail out with their shoes and hats, but water kept seeping in. By the time they were rescued none of them had the strength to even stand up. The sailors in the French fishing boat lifted them out of the lifeboat, one by one.

My grandfather, who was not supposed to grieve, was sent to stay with his cousins in Guernsey. But, clearly, he never stopped thinking about his mother, because he begged his father for a boat, as soon as he was old enough. His father, terrified of losing his last, remaining son, forbade him to sail at sea and only allowed him a small sailing boat on the Norfolk Broads.

As soon as his father died, he bought a small yacht and sailed to the Channel Islands, where his brother Claude's body, which washed up on the shore, was buried. He bought a house on Alderney and his whole family spent their summer holidays there while he kept his yacht in the harbour and sailed as often as he could. After he retired, he spent most of his time on the island, sailing away in all weathers. His mother's body, dragged down by her voluminous skirts, was never found. So, he would set off in fair weather and foul to the place where the Stella went down. Did he know he was searching for her or was it just a gut feeling that he had to be at sea? Or did he just want to be near her? I don't know. One day, rowing a dingy out to his yacht in the harbour, he had a heart attack and died. He died where he wanted to be, at sea, and he was buried in the little Alderney cemetery, next to his brother.

When the Stella was discovered by divers, the whole story came to the surface. We watched the video of her resurrection, with pictures of my grandfather, before and after the wreck, his beautiful blue eyes permanently changed to the sad eyes I remembered as a child, and we grieved and wept for his loss. Was this a healing process? I don't know, but I feel something changed for all of us.

There was another loss that touched me deeply: that of my uncle Robert, who died six months before I was born. He died fighting the Japanese, during the second world war. His body was buried where he fell, in Manipur, one of the North East States of India, a place that was once a Principality but became part of India after the second world war.

I became obsessed with tracing his war experiences, from Waziristan in the North West Frontier, to Manipur, fighting in the monsoon, drenched and muddy, only to fall, a few days before the Japanese surrender. I tried to travel to Manipur, to see the place where he died, but rioting broke out and I was prevented. He was another member of the family who was never mourned. No funeral, no coffin to lower down, no speeches praising his great deeds and lamenting his early death, no wake. Like so many who died in the second world war, he slipped away without leaving a trace, never to be mentioned again. Many who lost loved ones in France, travelled there to visit their graves in the great mass cemeteries, perhaps finding some solace.

Whole countries, such as Spain, have been traumatised: in this case by the atrocities of Franco, whose death squads killed hundreds of thousands of victims in mass executions during the White Terror. For many years after Franco's death people campaigned for the exhumation of the mass graves, but the government that followed Franco refused, saying that it was better to forget all about it. Eventually a few men formed The Association for the Recovery of Historical Memory, an organisation that collects testimonies about Franco's White Terror and excavates and identifies bodies from mass graves. It is now a group of about fifty archeologists, anthropologists and forensic scientists. They identify the remains using DNA tests and other forensic methods. By October 2009 they had identified 1,700 victims. This was a drop in the ocean of people killed by Franco's death squads and their work was hampered by the refusal of the Rajoy Government to give them access to the archives which would indicate precisely where the mass graves lie. If the Spanish people are to heal, they need to find the bones of the executed, to bury them with all due ceremony.

Worldwide the disappearance of people causes unending anguish, can haunt societies for generations and tear the social fabric of the community in which the missing people lived. Chile, El Salvador, Haiti, Argentina, Bolivia, Colombia, Costa Rica, Ecuador, El Salvador, Guatemala, Mexico, Nicaragua, Panama, Peru, Venezuela, are just a few of the countries where tens of thousands of people have disappeared without trace. Their relatives continue to cry out, desperate to know whether they are alive or dead. If they are dead, they need to know where they are buried and to have proof of their death so that they can start to grieve. They live in the grip of constant anguish, intent on a search that they will not give up until they know what has happened to their loved ones.

The world became aware of forced disappearances during the right-wing military dictatorships which governed most Latin American countries during the 1970s and 1980s. Without dead bodies, these governments could deny knowledge of people's whereabouts and any accusations that they had been killed.

After the Argentinian military dictatorship ended, investigations estimated that about 30,000 people were forcefully disappeared. Many of their bodies were dropped into the sea from airplanes. In Pinochet's Chilean dictatorship 3,200 people disappeared. Their bodies were buried in mass graves in the Atacama Desert. Their ageing family members still walk there, searching for bone fragments. The Truth Commission into El Salvador's civil war reported more than 8,000 people disappeared. In Peru 16,000 people disappeared and were probably buried in more than 6,000 unmarked graves. 45,000 people disappeared in Guatemala. The numbers are necessarily imprecise because there were no corpses, no traces, no explanations and therefore no accountability. The verb 'to disappear' has been transformed into an intransitive verb: to be disappeared, which is itself an awkward and incomplete mode of expression, communicating the involuntary nature of a person's disappearance. The disappeared are neither dead nor alive, neither present nor absent.

Gradually social movements, predominantly composed of women, arose in Latin America. In 1977, in Argentina, Mothers of Plaza de Mayo began marching at the Plaza de Mayo in Buenos Aires, in front of Argentina's presidential palace, demanding the return of their children. They wore white head scarves to symbolise the diapers of their lost children. The women created an unexpected force and their protests drew world attention to the disappeared. In Guatemala the Mutual Support Group was founded in 1984. When the Argentinian dictatorship fell, the new government launched a National Commission on Disappeared Persons (CONADEP) to try to account for the disappeared and accorded them the status of forced disappearance. The state finally admitted responsibility. The government began collecting testimony about the disappeared and in 1985 began prosecuting the criminals, starting with the Trial of the Juntas. Unfortunately, this came to an end until Kirchner came to power and started them again. Fewer than 600 people's remains have been found and identified by the Forensic Anthropology Team in Argentina. However, more recently Fabian Magnotta collected accounts from islanders in the Parana Delta, who found bodies washed up onto the banks of the Delta. He compiled these accounts into a book about the Death Flights which threw prisoners from planes during the military dictatorship. After publication of his book many more people came forward with accounts of bodies they had found. Families of the disappeared now hope that the remains of their loved ones can be found.

Human Rights organisations trying to find out where the disappeared have been buried in Latin America are sometimes prevented from accessing valuable information by the amnesty laws granted to the military after the end of the dictatorships, such as those in Guatemala and El Salvador. Some of the files documenting the atrocities have been granted secret statuses.

The Latin American Federation of the Detained Disappeared, FEDEFAM was formed to gather reports of forced disappearances, to help member Associations to search, and publish information, to promote international solidarity and to provide psychological and social assistance to the relatives of the disappeared. FEDEFAM represents the people of Latin America who seek justice and truth and commemorates the courage of those who searched for their loved ones and who resist oblivion. The organisation celebrates the trials that continue to take place in spite of a legacy of terror and impunity that seeks to silence the demands for justice. Social healing requires accountability, and accountability requires evidence. The families of the disappeared need to find the bones of their loved ones, so that they can lay them to rest in accordance with the rites and rituals of their cultural, social and religious traditions. FEDEFAM campaigned for an International Day of Enforced Disappearances, to commemorate all the victims of forced disappearances, and in 2010 United Nations declared August 30th International Day of Enforced Disappearances.

Sadly, enforced disappearances continue in Latin America, now often linked with drug trafficking. Since 2006 30,000 Mexicans have gone missing and about 70,000 more have been killed. The poet Javier Sicilia planned to march alone from Cuernavaca to Mexico City in protest after his son's murder; 150,000 people joined him.

Where evidence is difficult to obtain, memory can go a long way towards helping society to heal. In Santiago, Chile, a Museum of memory has been built to create visual and public accountability for the regime's crimes.

Another approach to healing this tragedy is through art. The Colombian sculptor Doris Salcedo has long worked on her subject: her Atrabiliarios series uses shoes to represent the missing. Noemi Escandell's 'Disappeared' depicts an empty-armed Pieta wearing one of the kerchiefs of the Mothers of the Paza de Mayo. The Argentinian photographer Gustavo Germano, whose brother was disappeared, recreates decades-old family photos, retaking the image with only the surviving family members. Mixing performance art with political theatre, the group HIJOS, representing the children of the disappeared, stage noisy guerrilla protests, outside the homes of accused perpetrators.

People have disappeared throughout the world, including Africa and Asia. Forced disappearance is not just a problem for the victims and their families but of the countries affected and indeed the whole world. Societies cannot be constructed on a foundation of false reconciliation, inadequate justice, presidential pardons and forgetting injustices done.

Thousands of refugees lie at the bottom of the Mediterranean, leaving their relatives traumatised by their untimely deaths. The disappearance of people is a global phenomenon, caused by wars, migration, dictatorships, accidents and earthquakes, in all cases leaving the survivors in need of healing. It may not always be possible to find the bones of the disappeared, especially if they lie at the bottom of the sea, but they need to be honoured in the way that is most appropriate to the people who have lost their loved ones.

Angela Paine runs workshops on Celtic medicinal plants and is the author of *Healing Power of Celtic Plants* and *Healing Plants of the Celtic Druids*.

Saving the Tinkers' Heart

Fiona Tinker

There is no more apposite an introduction to the Tinkers' Heart than this piece I wrote for our website:

> *In a small, quiet spot in Argyll, at a place where three roads meet, lies a heart made from white quartz. This is the Tinkers' Heart: a space sacred to Scotland's Travelling people.*
>
> *It is a place of love, of loss and of memory. It is a place where marriages were made, where children were named and where those Travelling men who lost their lives in wars were remembered.*
>
> *It is a place of both ancestors and descendants; where the past, the present and the future merge on the three roads.*
>
> *Travellers in times past walked the earth lightly and their sacred spaces have always been hidden in plain view. That sacred place was simply the landscapes they passed through.*

The Tinkers' Heart is such a little monument, a mere thumb print on the landscape of Scotland. Yet its importance, and the importance of what these white stones represent, cannot be over-emphasised. The Tinkers' Heart now lies in a field off the A815 Strachur to Cairndow road, which runs along the side of Loch Fyne. The base to apex road is Hell's Glen Road, leading to Lochgoilhead or to The Rest and Be Thankful, on the road to Arrochar.

Once though, these old roads were main thoroughfares and a meeting on the road was a meeting at the Tinkers' Heart. It lay on the passage through Campbell land; and the Laird and his Lady were fiercely proud and protective of both the Heart and the Tinkers – the Scottish Travellers – who passed through. Time changes things though and with time came a change in landowner.

To add to the Heart's trouble, a new road was built in the 1970s to accommodate increasing motorised traffic. The new road was realigned and the Tinkers' Heart bypassed. The Heart remained at the junction of the remains of the three old roads whilst a busier, faster world got on with its own business a few hundred feet away.

But what is this Heart about? It begins as an oral story, one handed down through generations. The intersection of the three roads was a meeting point before 1746. After this time, it became a quiet monument to those Traveller men who lost their lives at Culloden, as the survivors and their families fled the repercussions of that battle. Many Clansmen and their kin joined with the Travellers, becoming itinerants in their quest to stay alive. The Heart's white quartz stones were the keepers of memory and memorial to those lost to death or transportation. It's not hard to imagine how forlorn and unhappy such a place of weeping could become.

But Scottish Travellers are survivors and life must – and does – go on. The Tinkers' Heart saw happier times as Scottish Travellers gathered there to celebrate marriages and new babies, whilst also honouring their dead. The marriages conducted at the Tinkers' Heart in the presence of only witnesses were legal, no minister or priest was required. They were deemed 'irregular' marriages but they were no less valid for that and children of these unions were legitimate.

Historically, there were four forms of marriage in Scotland, one regular and three irregular. A regular marriage was conducted by a Church of Scotland Minister, banns would be called for three Sundays prior to the marriage and the marriage details entered into the parish register – if the minister remembered. There was (and still is) no requirement for a marriage to take place in a church or similar in Scotland. It was (and still is) a person who is authorised to conduct a regular marriage and many of these authorised regular marriages took place in people's homes or places of their choosing.

A common form of 'irregular' marriage was a Declaration of Marriage in front of witnesses, without the presence of a minister. Such witnessing confirmed the validity of the marriage and there was no need for official involvement. Although frowned on by the establishment, these marriages suited those not of the established church – and those who preferred to have as little to do with authority as possible. Thus, the Tinkers' Heart, developed as a place to celebrate life and survival, also became a place of ceremony for Tinkers' Weddings. There is an old saying: 'Remember those from whom you come.' The sense of that, in knowing where you come from, who you are and where you are going is mirrored in the liminal space at the intersection of the three roads. The triple spiral of past, present and future turns in its never-ending cycle of birth, death and rebirth with the Heart as its centre.

The second form or irregular marriage was that of a Marriage by Promise, followed by sexual intercourse. This Promise had to be evidenced; either in the form of a letter or as an oath sworn before witnesses. This was a form of marriage that seems more suited to the settled community where a couple may have wished to escape parental disapproval. It also required a level of literacy that was unlikely to apply to the majority of Scottish Tinkers at that time.

One further interesting thing about the irregular marriages was that, should they choose to, couples could apply for a sheriff's warrant to have their marriage registered by licence of the Sheriff. Given that the couples were considered legally married, their children legitimate and all had the same inheritance rights as 'regular' married couples, it is a possibility that not too many couples were bothered about the form of their marriage, at least until they had other legalities to deal with that required proof of marriage.

By 1834, the law changed, permitting officiants from other religions to conduct regular marriages. However, there still was no civil marriage in the sense we understand today. The two irregular forms above were ways round this for those who did not wish to marry in a religious ceremony for whatever reason.

According to statistics from Glasgow University, from around 1870 to 1914 12% of all registered marriages in Scotland were 'irregular'. The two forms of irregular marriage discussed above were made illegal in 1939 and in July 1940, civil marriage in a registry office was introduced.

However, the third form of 'irregular' marriage was not abolished until 2006 – this was marriage by habit and repute; i.e. a couple presenting as married and who were, for all intents and purposes, married under common law. Scotland now has both marriage forms: religious and civil. But – whatever form they take – they all now have to be written in a marriage schedule and recorded by the local registry offices; thus, they are all 'regular' marriages.

Going back to a time where Scotland's Travelling folk lived their lives with as little contact with authorities as could be helped, it is easy to see why the Tinkers' Heart became a focus and a gathering place for the rites of passage in life. To stand by the Heart is to stand in a liminal space and in the presence of those who walked that way beforehand. The sacredness of the spot beats in the earth underfoot and is carried in the wind and the water. By keeping memory at the Tinkers' Heart, naming bairns, marrying and mourning the recently departed; Travellers showed respect to the memories and sacrifices of the men and women who suffered so much after Culloden. It could be argued that a Marriage by Declaration in front of witnesses at this place of ancestors had more solemnity of promise and intent than a 'regular' marriage. Though few of these marriages were recorded officially, the Travellers' *seanchaidhean* – the storytellers / historians – could (and still do) rattle off genealogies, family connections and old gossip in a way that would cause massive envy in a Druid in training.

In the light of the above, one would think that such an important place would have recognition and be a place of celebration, given its role and importance in the story of Scotland's Travelling People. Sadly, this was not the case and the Heart became somewhat isolated in its field. Matters were made worse by the present landowner renting the field to a famer who used it for his cattle. The Heart was in serious danger of becoming trampled into the mud.

However, many people still remembered the Tinkers' Heart and what it stood for. One of them was author and story-teller, Jess Smith. She is a Scottish Traveller who writes about her life growing up on the road and who records some of the tales of Tinkers from the past. Jess's mother was born on the shores of Loch Fyne, just under the Heart and the place is a sacred place of reverence for Jess.

Jess was disturbed by the state of the place, particularly when she found the Heart covered by wooden pallets as 'protection' against the herd of Highland Cattle wandering about it. She began a campaign to try to save the Heart and got in contact with several local luminaries; as well as Argyll and Bute Council and Michael Russell MSP. The local heritage organisation at Cairndow was also interested – the Heart was an important wee place to many of the locals too. Eventually, an iron fence was erected around the Heart to keep the kye from trampling the stones. In cow terms though, it was still flimsy, but it was better than nothing.

A chance meeting with Jess in 2013 led to a conversation about the Tinkers' Heart – a place I'd known many years. She told me what she'd achieved so far and how much of a battle it had been to get to that point. Right from the beginning, she had the solid backing of Mike Russell; the MSP for that part of Scotland. With his help, Jess had made some headway in having the Heart protected. However, there were disputes and the possibility that the Heart could be irretrievably damaged by cattle or quarrying if nothing was done officially to ensure it was recognised as a place of importance in the story of Scotland and her people.

From our conversation a campaigning group, The Heart of the Travellers (HOTT) was born. Our aim was to save the Heart by having it scheduled as a monument of national importance and to gain recognition for the culture of Scottish Travellers.

The Scottish Government has a system of Petition, where people can bring their complaints directly to a government committee if enough signatures are collected at the initial petitioning stage. HOTT decided that a direct approach to our Parliament at Holyrood would be the best way of highlighting our concerns. Between us, we composed our petition (No. PE1523) and uploaded it to the Scottish Government's website in 2014.

The response to this petition was astounding. Many, many people knew about the Tinkers' Heart through their families, Travellers and settled alike, and the support our petition received was amazing. It became a bit like Topsy and just grew and grew. Our campaign group developed a website and an online magazine. Jess was nominated as spokeswoman –she's excellent at public speaking – and there were press interviews, public meetings and events held to discuss and support the Heart.

HOTT was then invited to present our case to a committee at Parliament. Six of us attended, but only Jess was permitted to speak in her role as HOTT's spokesperson. The rest of us sat behind her and listened as she presented our case as to why this little Heart of Quartz should be given protected status. She was professionalism personified, presenting our case, answering all questions and not once, in the hour and a half we were there, faltering in the face of opposition. Frankly, she was incredible – her knowledge, passion for the Heart and for the culture of

Scottish Travellers shone from her.

However, passion is not always enough. It needs determination to see it through and in this case, we needed a good dose of it. Our petition to have the Tinkers' Heart scheduled was initially refused as it did not quite fit with the criteria then used to award Historic Monument status.

Although this was disappointing, we saw it as a bump in the road. Our supporters – including several MSPs – were vocal in their disappointment and we appealed the decision. It is important to emphasise that the initial refusal was procedural – a decision could only be based on the regulations in use at that time. And that became the basis of the appeal – perhaps the regulations need to be looked at to account for intangible heritage?

The Petitions Committee and Historic Environment Scotland (HES) reconsidered our petition. HES launched a consultation to research the Tinkers' Heart. HES worked incredibly hard, travelling all over Scotland to speak with people who could tell them stories of the Heart. They investigated what written records there are. Their work was thorough and spread over many months. Mike Russell was, as always, stalwart in his support, as were several other MSPs, HES and media broadcasters such as Frieda Morrison and Breege Smyth. Supporters from both the Travelling and the settled communities gave so much of themselves to convince the Petitions Committee to reconsider. We even had a song written for us. And it worked.

Whatever the Heart meant on a personal level to all the individuals who gathered to help save it for future generations, they all gathered because of the love of the place. The Heart beat strong.

In June 2015, we received news from HES, via a letter written to the Petitions' Committee, which informed them that Historic Environment Scotland had reviewed the way in which they processed information gathered and that their lengthy reinvestigation changed their view of the Heart's importance:

> *On the basis of this new work, we now consider Tinkers' Heart is a site of high cultural significance in three main areas:*
>
> 1. *It gives us a great understanding of the traditions and material heritage of Scottish Travellers;*
> 2. *It is a rare example of a permanent physical monument of Scottish Travellers; and*
> 3. *It holds a high significance in the consciousness of Gypsy / Travellers and the people of Argyll as a symbol of Scottish Travellers and their heritage.*
>
> *In the light of this, we intend to place Tinkers' Heart on the Schedule as a monument of national importance.*

(Extract from a letter to the Petitions Committee from Barbara Cummins, Director of Heritage Management, HES, 18th June, 2015.)

The effects of scheduling – of having the Tinkers' Heart added to the list of monuments of national importance is a huge step in securing its future. It gives the site recognition and protection. It acknowledges the paths of those who came before us. And it places the Tinkers' Heart firmly in the weave of the story of Scotland and its people.

But HOTT's work is not yet done. We have plans for the site, which need to be made in agreement with all parties concerned. Our vision is to have the area around the Tinkers' Heart transformed from a cow field into a place of quiet reflection, perhaps surrounding the stones with a three-walled drystane dyke with seating and lots of native flowering plants. The path to the Heart – part of the old Hell's Glen Road – is in dire need of attention. The metal cage surrounding the Heart is, at the moment, a necessary eyesore. That can't be removed until the cows have a new field.

These are plans for the future of the Heart and both HOTT

and the local settled community know it cannot stop at just having the site scheduled.

The final words about the Tinkers' Heart belong to the past, to the protection of the Heart and to the power of memory held in white quartz, as expressed in this old blessing:

Clocha , clocha beag , o clocha beag bán
Cosúil go bhfuil cnámha an domhain d'aois tú
Cosúil leis an easnacha mar gheall ar an croí a bhfuil tú.
Cosain an áit seo áit a bhfuil mé ag seasamh
I gcás go bhfuil sé ar an áit ina luíonn tú faoi láthair.

Stones, little stones, o little white stones
Like the earth's old bones are you
Like the ribs about the heart you are.
Protect this place where I am standing
For it is the place where you lie presently.

The Tinkers' Heart is beating strongly again. In that sacred place, in those beats lie the memories of our ancestors, our love of now and our hopes for the future.

Fiona Tinker has taught English to secondary school pupils, in both England and Scotland, for over twenty years. She is actively involved in civic advocacy work in Scotland and is the author of *Pathworking through Poetry* and *Stories for the Songs of the Year*.

Schism & Split: Wounds that can never heal

Mélusine Draco

Traditional witchcraft means different things to different people. According to the late Michael Howard, the term applies to 'any non-Gardnerian, non-Alexandrian, non-Wiccan or pre-modern form of the Craft, especially if it has been inspired by historical forms of witchcraft and folk magic'. Another definition was offered by Daniel A. Schulke of Cultus Sabbati, when he proclaimed that traditional witchcraft:

> refers to a coterie of initiatory lineages of ritual magic, spell-craft and devotional mysticism ... [sharing] a common feature of extreme selectivity when it comes to prospective members, and the willingness to reject those proven unfit for the work.

These differences are nothing new. A few decades ago (pre-social media), a large number of neo-pagans insisted on referring to themselves as 'white witches', much to the derision from more traditional practitioners. No doubt they felt that this appellation allayed any suspicion of wrong-doing but this misrepresentation had a serious backlash. By claiming a 'white' label for themselves in their pursuit of herbalism and crystal-healing they set up the media guidelines for accusations of evil against anyone whom they felt might be slightly more 'greyer' than themselves. And believe it or not, some of those 'white' witches were among the first to publicly point the wand at those whose traditions were older, deeper and duskier than the pagan revivalists were willing to accept.

The burgeoning 'satanic survivors' accounts added to the considerable amount of suspicion surrounding Craft of the 1980-90s with tales of ritualized sex, drug taking and child abuse; with all the 'survivors' freely admitting taking part in devil worship. Because of the lack of factual information, the public were willing to accept such survivors' revelations as genuine, especially when they were endorsed by statements from registered charities, social services, politicians and clergy. Scaremongering began channeling attention to the modern defender of the hearth – the mother who was constantly bombarded with stories that her own children were under threat from perverted followers of Satan who lurked around every corner. These seemingly ordinary and respectable women were cunningly utilized as unguided missiles to be launched against pagans and occultists to break up occult fayres, disrupt spiritualist meetings, attack local witches in supermarkets, and prevent customers from entering occult shops.

In April 1988, the anti-occult campaign began in earnest with an astounding outburst in the House of Commons, which singled out, named, misrepresented and slandered the Sorcerer's Apprentice:

In the city of Leeds can be found a flashmail order centre of the Sorcerer's Apprentice. Just up the hill is the large store called Astonishing Books under the same control. This business is founded on books on witchcraft, black magic, satanic rituals, and other occult practices ... It is common knowledge that witchcraft initiation rituals involve the abuse of children ...'

Later, fanatics broke into Astonishing Books, smashing bookshelves containing books on witchcraft, Satanism and Aleister Crowley. They made a pile of these books, and these alone, in the centre of the shop, poured petrol over them, fired it and left, taking nothing else.

It was, therefore, entirely without warning in the spring of 1988 that the Sorcerer's Apprentice became the focus for a concerted and highly inflammable (no pun intended) three-year campaign to destroy occultism at source. The scare-mongers had prepared their infamous *dossier* with the help of several quisling pagans, who had provided a valuable insight into the contemporary pagan scene, naming names, magazines, shops and organizations. In reality, this dossier was no more than a potted listing of UK businesses, publications and individuals – but it was used by anti-occult campaigners as evidence of the upsurge in witchcraft – which they considered to be the same as Satanism.

The campaign lasted five years and successfully tricked not only the British public into believing that satanic ritualised child-abuse really existed, but quite a few uninformed pagans, too! It was quickly discovered that the dividing line between gullible fundamentalists and gullible pagans was extremely vague, and for the duration of the campaign it was also revealed that several self-righteous pagans had helped the anti-occult campaigners' cause by supplying background information and incorrect opinions, thereby supporting the persecution and jeopardizing other pagans, whist safeguarding themselves from attack. There were those who firmly believed that *all* pagans should stand up and be counted because this anti-occult campaigning played on fears and prejudices. The Minister for Local Government, Michael Howard, however, defended the decision of ordinary pagans not to come out of the closet despite the fact that such shy behavior was condemned by those who had already taken the giant leap into the public limelight

But out of those prejudices rose the *oriflame* of occultism and entered the lists as its champion. Those who had followed the victimisations from the beginning looked upon the fire-bombing as the last straw and spontaneously sent in cash to help rebuild the damaged shop. The cash, however, was put into a fund to pay for legal costs incurred in combating satanic hysteria. That idea formalised into the Sub-Cultural Alternatives Freedom Foundation (SAFF), which grass-roots members more fondly remember as the Sorcerer's Apprentice Fighting Fund. This swiftly grew into a national organisation set up and financed by thousands of people (and not all of them pagan), to protect their freedom of belief.

By March 1990 the SAFF was in a position to bring court action against people who infringed those rights and to offer specialist legal advice to those who suffered harassment. For the first time in history, pagans didn't need to suffer persecution by vicious neighbours or bigoted employers because they didn't have the financial resources to fight back. It had a massive data base of information, photographs, tape recordings, news clippings, documents and other research resources that would normally have taken years to compile. From all over the country copies of radio tapes, newspaper cuttings and information were flooding in to ensure that no article or interview that misrepresented occultism was allowed to pass without some form of complaint being registered against the editor or programme makers. Fortunately for British paganism, the police were not dragged into this whirlpool of fanaticism and fantasy ... but despite the efforts of SAFF, the Pagan Federation and various other individuals, there were also a series of media performances by some pagans that were downright detrimental to Craft.

The tide began to turn on 12th August 1990, when *The Independent on Sunday* ran Rosie Waterhouse's 'The Making of a Satanic Myth' which refused to swallow any more fundamentalist prating without any evidence to support the claims. The Rochdale scandal broke in the newspapers at the beginning of September, revealing that children had been snatched from their beds at 7am in the morning and placed in care; the parents subsequently silenced by injunctions that prevented them talking about their experiences to anyone outside the court. On 9th September *The Mail on Sunday* unleashed its own indignant attack by running a double-page spread, emphasising the plight of the families involved. It was a breakthrough for paganism, but far too late to prevent the misery inflicted on innocent families, since the majority of the accused parents had no more occult interest than watching the late-night horror movie, or reading the latest James Herbert bestseller!

Finally, common sense prevailed when the so-called overwhelming evidence for all these social misdemeanors was found to be non-existent. Following the Report of the inquiry into child abuse in Cleveland (1987) prepared by Judge Elizabeth Butler-Sloss and the findings of Professor Jean la Fontaine (*The Extent and Nature of Organised and Ritual Abuse* 1994), the 'satanic child-abuse myth' evaporated almost overnight. Ironically, an earlier 1960s anti-occult campaign rooted very firmly in rural England had quickly floundered with relatively few casualties among pagan folk – but that, too, had also sunk without trace. The 1980s anti-occult campaign, however, had produced an unexpected victim – the integrity of the pagan community itself:

[This] anti-occult campaign has revealed a completely new perspective on occultism in this country, both from without and within. The continuous crisis that threatened the community, separated the genuine from the pseudo and underlined the real lack of real commitment in some of the self-styled pagan leaders ... fundamentalism [may] have done occultism a favour in that the popularization of paganism in recent years had spawned many pseudo and soft-underbellies; yuppy-occultists who are themselves misled and who subsequently mislead others. [Malleus Satani]

The SAFF may have formed a hard-core nucleus of committed activists but it also exposed the lack of commitment on the part of many senior British practitioners. Even well-known authors receiving royalties from their publications and inciting others to follow their teachings, refused to defend their own writings when the going got rough. They had seen occult publishers, openly defamed by the fundamentalist press, refuse to get involved despite the fact that pagan books provided them with their incomes. There were 'three dozen well-known occultists who turned and ran', or otherwise complicated the already complex proceedings in order to save their own jobs or reputation, which they apparently considered had priority over their integrity.

During the spring of 1989, *The Pipes of Pan* published a hard-hitting article entitled 'Divided We Stand – Divided We Fall' that questioned the apathy of fellow-Crafters. Not only did the writer criticize those who backed away from the threat, but delivered a sharp rebuke to those who disparaged the efforts of others who *did* attempt to defend their faith. The prognosis warned that Craft, was in danger of going the same way as the Christian Church, into schism and split.

While those spearheading the counter-attack accused others of 'plastic paganism', moderates objected to the big boots and boxing gloves approach of those carrying the fight to the very doorsteps of the Establishment; both sides adamant that theirs was the only way to promote understanding and acceptance of their faith. One would assume that with the 'satanic child-abuse' myth gathering momentum that all pagans would have branded together to defend themselves against such allegations.

This proved not to be the case; some even publicly dismissed Social Services' dawn roundups of children as none of their concern, because the majority of cases did not affect anyone with genuine pagan involvement. Several *pagan* publications even stated that as far as they were aware, there had been *no* cases of pagan children being taken into care – or worse – nor even any 'unprovoked investigations.' This was incorrect – there *had* been cases of pagan children being taken into care as the ever-growing SAFF files showed and several parents lost custody cases because of their pagan beliefs. In fact, the authorities had successfully gagged parents by lawful process, which prevented any of them from contacting organisations such as the SAFF for help and that was why no details surrounding the cases were made public.

Another aspect of the division between different factions was neo-paganism becoming so far removed from its roots based on anthropology/mythology rather than on its magical perspectives. In 1964 Robert Cochrane [*The Craft Today*], revealed that even then there were those whose motives were suspect:

> *It would appear that the Craft has rapidly become an escape hatch for all those who wish to return to a more simple form of life and escape from the ever-increasing burden of contemporary society. In many cases the Craft has become a funk-hole, in which those who have not been successful in solving various personal problems hide.*

Michael Howard felt that the basic problem with the public image of the occult in general and Craft in particular, was that it was totally alien to the average person, especially the orthodox church-goer.

> *This is partly because most people have alienated themselves from their psychic roots and Nature, and partly because of the image which many witches promote publicly. There are beliefs and practices which your average person will never understand – and it may not even be feasible to bother to educate them!*

In an open letter to readers if the *Lamp of Thoth* magazine, he outlined the cruel, hard facts concerning trafficking with the media:

> *Personally I have no wish either to be associated with the many self-appointed spokespersons who claim to represent the Old Ways in the public eye ... Anyone who believes they can have editorial control over interviews or news stories after the journalist involved leaves their home is, quite frankly, loving in cloud-cuckoo-land ... Because of the high profile of this type of person, they tend to attract*

media coverage because basically they make a good story. That is all the average media hack is ultimately after. Journalists do not give a shit about the spiritual aspects of the Old Ways and – to be honest – neither do many (not all, of course) of the witches and pagans they interview. [Malleus Satani]

Meriem Clay-Egerton was also quick to criticize those media-witches whom, she said, appear giving their impression that they are armed with a yard-brush and a never-emptying cauldron of whitewash for the Craft. As a witch, she added, she rather objected to having such an apologetic attitude taken on behalf of witchcraft:

If 'modern' wet-behind-the-ears, eco-obsessed neo-pagans wish to proclaim a belief in living an unnatural kiddies fairy story, more power to their imagination, but please don't try to make the general public, or newcomers, think that this is all there is to the Craft.

Thirty years later those schisms have never completely healed – and they never will. Because whether the pagan community like to admit it or not – there are now *two* distinct approaches to witchcraft. One is the cleaned up, politically correct, socially acceptable form of neo-goddess worship with little, or no mention of the god, since his image is more difficult to render impotent. Unfortunately, this is increasingly becoming the generalized public face of witchcraft because traditionalists who prefer not to sanitise their deities, have retreated back into the shadows through sheer exasperation at the trivialization of their beliefs. The traditional approach to deity acknowledges the dual importance of both male *and* female elements which is essential to effective magical working.

There are few apologists among the ranks of the traditionalists, who appear less frequently on television and, more often than not, decline to give interviews for the national press decked out in flowing robes with garlands of flowers and pointy hats. Traditionalists often present a darker, less benign countenance – and it is towards this image of traditional of Craft that neo-pagans point the accusing finger of being practitioners of 'black magic'.

The occult revival of the 1970s, which began as an intelligent, almost scientific investigation of the supernatural, now appears to have taken second place to a rebirth of superstition. Today's esoteric reader wants sound-bites, scrappy bits of information that enables them to pass themselves off as knowledgeable members of the pagan community. There is also a concern about the watered-down versions of paganism that appear to be the only reading material now available which, to quote Dion Fortune, isn't paganism but decomposing Christianity. Nowadays, if we want serious books on magical subjects, we've got to know where to look and, as a result, the prices of many reliable collector's books are no longer affordable.

Despite the graphic claims of the tabloid press, anti-occult campaigners and pagan apologists, gratuitous sex and magic *don't* mix. If we're not given the complete facts, we never really know the truth but in an expose of New World Wicca posted on the internet last year, a lengthy polemic slammed the alleged sexual abuse within neo-paganism on their side of the pond. The author claimed to have run the whole gamut of pagan experience over a *twenty-year* period but had no experience or insider knowledge of any *British* Traditions – Wiccan or otherwise. Yet they had no compunction in using archive photographs of British 'skyclad' coven workings to suggest that all that was wrong in New World paganism could be traced back to good old Blighty, thereby making libelous claims against *living* witches. You cannot libel the dead but three of the most maligned were venerable elders with the British community and respected by those in Craft for keeping the faith down through the years.

Predatory males *and females* are nothing new – both within

Craft and without – and the pagan camps of the 1970s were a celebration of the new-found freedom of expression of the time; a revival of good old-fashioned, medieval paganism. The AIDS pandemic cooled things down quite considerably but there was a different morality back then – both within Craft and without. Nevertheless, those traditionalists among us who have considerably more than twenty-year's experience under our collective Old Craft cords strongly object to accusations leveled against those who were fully-fledged witches when the writer of this so-called expose was still in nappies.

As a self-proclaimed initiate, the author has probably broken just about every oath ever made because when a witch ritually affirms their pledge, via initiation, they are acquiring the full powers of the Craft and the Ancestors, and they reap the reward of *every* action. In this long and involved saga, it was obvious that our 'disgruntled witch' has made many poor life-choices and now wanted to shift the blame elsewhere to prove a point, because there is an unwritten law that what happens in Craft stays in Craft.

The most frightening aspect of history repeating itself, however, was the announcement in the *Irish Times* in January 2018 that 'Irish people are being ravaged by demonic possession', and that the Catholic Church was 'out of touch with reality' as they are sending sufferers of possession to psychologists instead of performing rituals! The Catholic News Agency in Rome reported demonic possessions were on the rise in Italy, despite *Vatican News* claiming that many Christians no longer believe in [the devil's] existence ... and when the church is in a position of weakness it requires a scapegoat.

It's happened twice before in living memory and it can happen again ... and how many self-styled pagans will join the ranks of accusers? Is it any wonder that the 'Perfect Love and Perfect Trust' philosophy of neo-paganism can never be reconciled with the 'Trust None' approach of traditional witchcraft?

Mélusine Draco is an Initiate of traditional British Old Craft and the Khemetic Mysteries and author of a number of pagan titles including the popular *Traditional Witchcraft* series published by Moon Books. She was a SAFF activist during the SCRAM years.

MOON
BOOKS

PAGANISM & SHAMANISM

What is Paganism? A religion, a spirituality, an alternative belief system, nature worship? You can find support for all these definitions (and many more) in dictionaries, encyclopaedias, and text books of religion, but subscribe to any one and the truth will evade you. Above all Paganism is a creative pursuit, an encounter with reality, an exploration of meaning and an expression of the soul. Druids, Heathens, Wiccans and others, all contribute their insights and literary riches to the Pagan tradition. Moon Books invites you to begin or to deepen your own encounter, right here, right now.

If you have enjoyed this book, why not tell other readers by posting a review on your preferred book site.

Medicine for the Soul
The Complete Book of Shamanic Healing
Ross Heaven
All you will ever need to know about shamanic healing and how to
become your own shaman…
Paperback: 978-1-78099-419-2 ebook: 978-1-78099-420-8

Shaman Pathways – The Druid Shaman
Exploring the Celtic Otherworld
Danu Forest
A practical guide to Celtic shamanism with exercises and
techniques as well as traditional lore for exploring the Celtic
Otherworld.
Paperback: 978-1-78099-615-8 ebook: 978-1-78099-616-5

Traditional Witchcraft for the Woods and Forests
A Witch's Guide to the Woodland with Guided Meditations and
Pathworking
Mélusine Draco
A Witch's guide to walking alone in the woods, with guided
meditations and pathworking.
Paperback: 978-1-84694-803-9 ebook: 978-1-84694-804-6

Wild Earth, Wild Soul
A Manual for an Ecstatic Culture
Bill Pfeiffer
Imagine a nature-based culture so alive and so connected,
spreading like wildfire. This book is the first flame…
Paperback: 978-1-78099-187-0 ebook: 978-1-78099-188-7

Naming the Goddess
Trevor Greenfield
Naming the Goddess is written by over eighty adherents and
scholars of Goddess and Goddess Spirituality.
Paperback: 978-1-78279-476-9 ebook: 978-1-78279-475-2

Shapeshifting into Higher Consciousness
Heal and Transform Yourself and Our World with Ancient
Shamanic and Modern Methods
Llyn Roberts
Ancient and modern methods that you can use every day to
transform yourself and make a positive difference in the world.
Paperback: 978-1-84694-843-5 ebook: 978-1-84694-844-2

Readers of ebooks can buy or view any of these bestsellers by
clicking on the live link in the title. Most titles are published in
paperback and as an ebook. Paperbacks are available in traditional
bookshops. Both print and ebook formats are available online.

Find more titles and sign up to our readers' newsletter at
http://www.johnhuntpublishing.com/paganism
Follow us on Facebook at https://www.facebook.com/MoonBooks
and Twitter at https://twitter.com/MoonBooksJHP